"In her latest book, *Praying with Christ-Sophia,* Jann Aldredge-Clanton invites us all to stretch our spiritual imagination so that we can experience the sacred symbolism of Christ-Sophia through hymns and rituals. Designed for use in diverse communities of women, men, and children, the rituals are participatory, healing, and open to new experiences of faith. This original collection is an invitation to creative participation, a celebration of inclusive partnership."

Letty M. Russell
Professor of Theology,
Yale University Divinity School

"One of the creative religious movements of recent years is the rapid appearance of a Wisdom theology and spirituality. The understanding of Christ is being restored to its ancient roots in immanent divine Wisdom. Jann Aldredge-Clanton has provided us with helpful resources for living this Wisdom-Christ spirituality in liturgy and personal prayer."

Rosemary Radford Ruether,
Georgia Harkness Professor of Applied Theology,
Garrett-Evangelical Theological Seminary

"Praying with Christ-Sophia is marvelous; it is inviting, inclusive, tender, and transformative. A welcome gift for all who long to give expression through ritual, symbol, and song to what lies deep within. A wonderful book! Courageous and creative!"

James Conlon
Director and Chair, The Sophia Center
Author, *Earth Story, Sacred Story*

"Jann Aldredge-Clanton gives us eyes to see and ears to hear the beauty and power of our God as we pray with Christ-Sophia. Her christological insights, fresh images, respect for tradition, and delightful hymns, woven together in well-crafted services can nurture, stretch, and empower a wide variety of Christian communities.

"Familiar tunes, seasons, and texts root participants, while the inclusivity and diversity lure them beyond the divisions, prejudice, and narrowness that have plagued society and churches. This is not 'women's prayer' for small marginal groups: it is an invitation to mainline Christianity to more diligently and faithfully seek the Holy One always beyond the limitations of our words and images."

Sr. Martha Ann Kirk
Professor of Religious Studies,
University of the Incarnate Word

"Praying with Christ-Sophia is a wonderful faith celebration in words and music. For those of us who have longed for and tasted inclusivity in community and worship, Jann has provided a worship resource rich with images of everyday living as well as hope for our future as a faith community. What a gift to us: to speak and sing and dream with no need to edit out exclusivity! What a gift to offer worship planners a way to expand and celebrate our responses to God's peacemaking among us."

Glenda Fontenot
President of the Board,
Baptist Peace Fellowship of North America

"For those, like me, who were converted in head and heart to the biblical truth and importance of Christ-Sophia by Jann's previous book, *In Search of Christ-Sophia,* we now have something for our hands. I hold this book open as I follow its profound poetry and spiritual wisdom in my personal devotional life. And I have handed it to our worship service leaders and planners so they have a practical guide to incorporate a fuller image of God into our Sunday morning services.

"Our Baptist congregation has slowly, but most certainly, accepted the liberating feminine face of God. Now we are on the next journey, the one to Christ-Sophia. Praise God for such a theologically sound, emotionally satisfying, and spiritually fulfilling adventure into what God is doing today in reconciling male and female in God's image!"

Rev. Paul R. Smith, Pastor
Author, *Is It Okay to Call God "Mother?":
Considering the Feminine Face of God*

"Persons come to experiences of worship with a desperate need for healing and wholeness. Jann Aldredge-Clanton has penned words that live and breathe. Her litanies and prayers, rituals and symbols, reach into the depths of the spirit and soul. Her worship experiences of healing draw up emotions long buried and spirit longings long dormant. Her celebrations of newfound renewal bring joy from the abyss of human sorrow and mourning. Her hymns give voice to the honest and unfettered stirrings of the heart.

"This work will speak to the soul and restore the spirit of all who worship through these inclusive and intergenerational experiences. Used within faith communities as they seek genuine heart worship, Jann Aldredge-Clanton's divine imagery will be nurturing and empowering."

Rev. Kathy Manis Findley
President of Baptist Women in Ministry
Author, *Voices of Our Sisters*

"A new christology is emerging as the church moves into the twenty-first century, a christology that recognizes the humanity of Jesus as embodying both Word and Wisdom, male and female, the Christ-Sophia of God. *Praying with Christ-Sophia* is a collection of beautifully written prayers, hymns, and rituals in the spirit of this new christology. Jann Aldredge-Clanton not only uses inclusive language and images in which both women and men will feel comfortable, but through her poetry and verse she has breathed new life into old hymns.

"This book is steeped in Scripture and tradition, yet the translations are contemporary in tone. It is a book of energizing and Spirit-filled prayer that helps the reader mourn and heal from life's painful events as well as celebrate life's gifts and seasons. It is a prayerbook for the twenty-first century."

Margaret "Meg" Gloger
New Creation Ministry, Inc.

Praying with Christ-Sophia

SERVICES

FOR HEALING

AND RENEWAL

Jann Aldredge-Clanton

XXIII

TWENTY-THIRD PUBLICATIONS

Mystic, CT 06355

ACKNOWLEDGMENTS

My deep gratitude goes to my colleagues and friends at Twenty-Third Publications. Neil and Pat Kluepfel gave their enthusiastic support from the conception of this creation. Mary Carol Kendzia, my editor, contributed not only her artistic expertise but also her patient attention to details. Mary Carol's affirmation, excitement, and creative partnership kept my energy flowing through the final stages of the process. I have also appreciated working with Bill Holub, Gwen Costello, and Georgiann Burdette.

Several people contributed creative works to this collection. I wish to thank Melanie Ferguson for her poem "Whittling at the Underlying," Barbara J. Middleton for her poem "Birth-Rebirth," Karen Ivy for collaborating with me on the hymn "Praise Ruah, Spirit Who Gives Birth," and Sally Browder for collaborating on the hymn "Our Sister Saints." My appreciation also goes to Nancy Ellett Allison for her insightful critique of my manuscript.

In addition, I wish to acknowledge the use of the following works:
Scripture quotations are from the *New Revised Standard Version of the Bible* (Grand Rapids, Michigan: Zondervan Bible Publishers, 1990), and from *The Jerusalem Bible* (New York: Doubleday, 1966), except where noted from the *Revised Standard Version of the Bible* (Nashville: Thomas Nelson, Inc., 1972).

All music for the hymns is in public domain and was taken from the following hymnals:
The Baptist Hymnal (Nashville, Tennessee: Convention Press, 1991); *The Presbyterian Hymnal* (Louisville, Kentucky: Westminster/John Knox Press, 1990); and *Hymns for the Living Church* (Carol Stream, Illinois: Hope Publishing Company, 1974).

Twenty-Third Publications
185 Willow Street
P.O. Box 180
Mystic, CT 06355
(860) 536-2611
800-321-0411

ISBN 0-89622-697-2
Library of Congress Catalog Card Number 96-60419
Printed in the U.S.A.

DEDICATION

To my sister Anne,
who embodies the mutual love and power
of the Divine Sister

To the New Wineskins Community,
whose creative partnership and encouragement
served as Divine Midwife to this book:
Nancy Ellett Allison, Ashley Bailey, Harriet Boorhem, Anna Lou Brown,
Larry Brown, Laurel Chaput, Margaret Christensen, Dawn Darwin,
Mitzi Ellington, Linda Ericson, Jo Smith Ferguson, Melanie Ferguson,
Elizabeth Ferguson, Elizabeth Infinger, Karen Ivy, Kathy Jones, Jonna Kelley,
Sean Kelley, Barbara Middleton, Cheryl Sauve, Melissa Walker-Luckett,
Elizabeth Watson-Martin, Renee Woods

CONTENTS

INTRODUCTION

When I was a young girl, I felt called to be a missionary. In my time and place in the world, that was the only divine call girls could hear. "Called" was such an awe-inspiring, romantic word to an eleven-year-old. But that's what I believed I was: "called" to be a missionary. Years passed, and the call lost its romance as other romances came into my life.

But the call returned in an unexpected way and place. Out of curiosity I went with my best friend and English-professor colleague to the ordination of one of the first Baptist women in the South. The ordination service was in a large church in downtown Dallas, Texas. People filled the sanctuary, coming for a variety of reasons. Some, like me, came out of curiosity, some came to criticize, and some came to bless.

After listening to a brief sermon based on Paul's letter to the Ephesians describing Christ's breaking down of dividing walls, I witnessed the breaking down of a formidable wall. For the first time in my life, I saw a woman kneeling before the church as a long line of people—women as well as men— passed by to lay hands of blessing upon her. My childhood memories of ordinations were of men kneeling at the altar while other men filed by like soldiers to lay on hands and whisper some words of initiation. The message I internalized was that this was a male ritual of initiation, kept apart from female hands, female images, or female language.

Now something new was happening. A woman was receiving the divine blessing. From somewhere deep within my soul I felt the rightness of it. Tears streamed down my face as I made a solemn, silent vow to do all in my power to spread this truth I was discovering. I would write articles, teach, and persuade; I would give chapter and verse to support this truth of women's sacred reality.

The ordination service ended, and people started leaving the sanctuary to go to the reception in the church parlor. I sat transfixed, with no strength or will to leave this holy place. My friend turned to me and said, "Jann, one day we'll be going to your ordination!" I gave her a look of shock, stammering something like, "No way can I do this! I'll support others, but I don't have what it takes to be ordained. And I'm not sure I want to. I don't want all the struggle and criticism that I know would come. Besides, you know I just finished my Ph.D. in English. I didn't spend all that time and energy for nothing!"

Seven years later, November 24, 1985, my friend stood in the sanctuary of a Baptist church in Waco, Texas, to read the Old Testament text at my ordination service. The text was Habakkuk 2:2–3: "Write the vision; make it plain on tablets, so that a runner may read it. For there is still a vision for the appointed time; it speaks of the end, and does not lie. If it seems to tarry, wait for it; it will surely come, it will not delay." The vision was becoming a reality in my life. I had thought my task would be to affirm the vision for others, to defend the vision in clear, logical, exegetical treatises. But the gentle, compelling voice of Christ-Sophia (although at that time I did not know her name) kept calling me until the vision became flesh in me.

The woman whose ordination I had attended seven years before preached the sermon at my ordination. She proclaimed that I was "the vision made flesh, the vision that God indeed calls women to ordination." She admonished me to claim the authority of my calling to be "hope for many women who may be frightened to hear God's call and to become preachers of the Word." She assured me that most important of all, I was one of God's own ordained.

Now it was my turn to preach, to proclaim the Good News of liberation. Knees trembling and heart pounding, I stood before the congregation to tell my story of call and vision. I told them that as a young girl I was so fearful of public speaking that I refused several times to go to church camp to avoid giving the inevitable report to the church when I came back. And here I was standing before them, behind an imposing pulpit in a large sanctuary, there by some power beyond my own, proclaiming a call different from anything I had ever expected or imagined. I quoted Shakespeare's Hamlet speaking to the rational Horatio, "There are more things in heaven and earth than are dreamed of in your philosophy."

Then I knelt before the congregation, inviting all who wished to come forward to lay on hands of blessing. Women and men, ordained and unordained, Baptist and Methodist and Catholic and Presbyterian, adults and children—hundreds of grace-filled people came by with words and hands of blessing. Powerful feelings washed over my spirit like waves washing over rocks along the seashore. Hard places softened with tears of joy, and determination strengthened with tears of sadness over the hundreds of years my sisters had been denied this sacred blessing. I wept for my mother, faithful daughter of the church; I wept for my grandmother, Greek scholar. They were never given official sanction or blessing by the church. I wept for my sisters in all faiths who were still denied this blessing. At the same time waves of hope washed my soul, filling me with fresh faith to walk toward a new vision and giving me power to act to make the vision reality. I claimed the promise that "the one who began the vision in me would bring it to completion" (Philippians 1:6).

After the ordination service, a clear image came into my mind: I saw everyone in that service kneeling before the congregation to receive the divine blessing. From that moment on, my vision included breaking down walls between ordained and unordained, extending the blessing of ordination to all women and men. My experience of ordination was the most profound affirmation I had ever received. I longed for everyone to have this experience. I believe everyone has a sacred calling and thus should receive a divine blessing mediated through a faith community.

This strong conviction of the power of communities to bring healing and blessing through sacred rituals has led me to create the services in this book. Developed from the belief that all are created in the divine image with abundant creative gifts, these services invite all to participate as equals.

All of the services in this collection are intended to break down hierarchies and to heal wounds inflicted by oppressive institutions and traditions. Because of my strong belief in the power of sacred symbols to shape our values and actions, the symbols of divinity in these services suggest partnership in restoring all creation to beauty and freedom.

Sacred Symbols of Shared Power

Our sacred symbols reflect and shape our deepest values. Influencing our culture are images of the Greek Zeus, who capriciously wielded his thunderbolt against other gods and human beings; of the Greek Hera, who used passive-aggressive means to destroy her enemies; of the Hebrew Jehovah, whom the Israelites often claimed as power to destroy every living thing in enemy cities; of the Cross of Christ, misused for power to conquer during the Crusades.

Militaristic imagery abounds in such Christian hymns as "Onward, Christian Soldiers" and "Lead On, O King Eternal." Sermons extolling Jesus as "a real man," to counteract any suggestions of a meek and mild and gentle Jesus, still come from pulpits in our society. The symbol of God as father has often been distorted to give fathers unrestrained power over children, resulting in abuse and violence. The symbols of God as master and king, the over-emphasis on submissiveness in the image of the Virgin Mary, and the prevailing references to God as "he" give further sanction to a dominant-submissive world order. Through these sacred symbols we have sanctified an unhealthy, destructive culture.

Our world stands in need of deep healing. Individuals, institutions, and the whole earth cry out for healing. As we move into the twenty-first century, we are awakening to our self-destructive behavior. Violence against women, in the form of battering in the home and sexual harassment on the job, is gaining increasing attention and legislation. Ecologists' warnings that we are depleting the earth's resources and destroying our natural environment are growing louder.

Many institutions founded on dominant-submissive patterns are struggling to move toward participatory, integrated systems. People are increasingly recognizing the connection between justice and peace. Twentieth-century feminist literature has been exploring alternative ways of structuring society along the principle of shared power.

To support these life-affirming forces and to increase their power we need new theological paradigms. The way a society images deity reflects and shapes that society's ideology and practice. The gender of the deity especially influences the degree of gender equality and peace the society enjoys. In her book *Woman as Healer*, Jeanne Achterberg demonstrates that "only in those times when the reigning deity has had a feminine, bisexual, or androgynous nature have women been able to exercise the healing arts with freedom and power."[1] And in *The Chalice and the Blade*, author Riane Eisler examines prehistoric civilizations that centered on goddess-worship, discovering that they enjoyed peace and partnership.[2]

A theology of female and male in the divine image calls for the inclusion of both genders in divine symbolism. The female sacred symbol alone, just as the male sacred symbol, is insuf-ficient for imaging the fullness of creation and for bringing the kind of healing our society needs. A single-gender sacred symbolism is incomplete and limiting. And since sacred symbolism forms the foundation of our value system, we also need nonhuman divine imagery for the healing of the earth. Scripture is rich with these images, such as the eagle (Deuteronomy 32:11–12), bear (Hosea 13:8), mother hen (Matthew 23:37), light (Psalm 27:1), bread (John 6:35), rock (Is 26:4), rose, and lily of the valley (Song of Songs 2:1).

In this collection of services, the central sacred symbol is Christ-Sophia. I believe this symbol holds great potential for the movement from patriarchal to egalitarian societies. Christ-Sophia overcomes dualisms and makes equal connections between male and female, black and white, Jewish and Christian traditions, thus providing a model for a society in which all beings live in a partnership instead of a dominant-submissive relationship. While rooted in Judaeo-Christian Scripture and tradition, the symbol of Christ-Sophia offers new possibilities for wholeness.

New Testament writers link Jesus Christ to Wisdom, a feminine symbol of deity in the Hebrew Scriptures. Biblical wisdom literature describes Wisdom (*Hokmah* in Hebrew) as sister, mother, female beloved, hostess, preacher, liberator, and establisher of justice. *Hokmah* symbolizes creative, redemptive, and healing power. In their efforts to describe this same power in the risen Christ, the apostle Paul and other New Testament writers draw from the picture of Wisdom. Paul refers to Christ as the power of God and the Wisdom (*Sophia* in Greek) of God (1 Corinthians 1:24). Proverbs describes *Hokmah* as the way, the life, and the path to wisdom (Proverbs 4:11,22,26); the writer of the Gospel of John depicts Christ as "the way, and the truth, and the life" (John 14:6).

What Judaism said of personified Wisdom (*Hokmah*), Christian writers came to say of Christ. The Gospel of Matthew records Jesus' identifying with *Sophia* (Wisdom): "The Son of man came eating and drinking, and they say, 'Look, a glutton and a drunkard, a friend of tax collectors and sinners!' Yet Wisdom (*Sophia*) is vindicated by her deeds" (Matthew 11:19). Sophia christology pervades early Christian tradition. The connection of Christ with Sophia, who wills the wholeness and humanity of everyone, enabled the earliest Christian communities to become a "discipleship of equals."[3] (In my book *In Search of the Christ-Sophia: An Inclusive Christology for Liberating Christians*, I give a thorough explanation of the biblical and theological basis for the symbol of Christ-Sophia, as well as an application of this symbol to spirituality, social justice, and community.)

By symbolizing partnership, Christ-Sophia offers new possibilities for relationship. The name "Christ-Sophia" suggests a connecting bridge between Christianity and Judaism by linking Christ, the resurrected deity of the Christian Scriptures, and Wisdom (*Sophia*), a personification of deity in the Hebrew Scriptures. Christ-Sophia symbolizes the equal connection between male and female in that the name "Christ" has traditionally denoted male divinity, and "Sophia" denotes female divinity. Christ-Sophia links races connecting the Jewish Jesus to Wisdom in both ancient and hellenized Judaism and drawing from both Egyptian and Greek sacred symbols. Caitlin Matthews demonstrates how Sophia, in blending black and white, transcends other dualisms.[4]

In a book first published in 1937, Sergei Bulgakov, a Russian Orthodox theologian who worked to bring Sophia back into Christian teaching, said that we need to sweep away the dust of ages and to decipher the sacred script to reinstate the tradition of Sophia. "It is holy tradition which lays such tasks upon us. It is a call neither to superstitious idolatry, nor to rationalistic contempt, but rather to creative understanding and development. Our own particular time with its special revelations and des-tiny has a peculiar call to this task."[5] Bulgakov's words sound a prophetic call in our time just as surely as in his own. Our world stands in deep need of the healing that will come through the resurrection of the Sophia tradition.

A sacred symbol must take root in our imaginations as well as our intellects if it is to shape our value system. In order for Christ-Sophia to become the foundation for a new egalitarian culture, we need to go beyond biblical and theological explanation to ritual experience in community. Through the creative development and aesthetic experience of Christ-Sophia symbolism in worship, we will convert our imaginations. Our actions will also change as the artistic and sensual dimensions of liberating rituals permeate our whole beings.

The intent of this collection is to stimulate ritual experience based on sacred symbolism that supports shared power. The image of Christ-Sophia forms the foundation of this symbolism. Other symbols strive to balance the feminine and the masculine, as well as include nonhuman beings.

Where I have given more prominence to feminine references, it is for the purpose of converting our imaginations that have been so deeply engrained with masculine images of God. I agree with Mary Kathleen Speegle Schmitt that "until the feminine is revalued and women are seen as valuable in the image of the Divine, we are left with an imbalance of understanding of the godhead, and justice for women is still lacking."[6] Repetition of female sacred images is vital to this revaluing of the feminine. The ultimate end is a truly inclusive, gender-balanced divine symbolism.

Hymns and Ritual Experience

As I was growing up, hymns shaped my theology and spirituality more than sermons or Scripture or Sunday School lessons. My earliest memories of church are of singing along with the congregation, even before I could read the words in the hymnal. I memorized the words as I heard them. Though my family was amused, I saw nothing funny in singing, "O come let us outdoor him."

Among the first pieces of music I learned to play on the piano were hymns. When we visited my paternal grandparents, Papa Aldredge would wake us up in the morning singing old Gospel hymns, like "This World is Not My Home" and "When We All Get to Heaven." He accompanied himself on the piano, playing by ear, never having learned to read music. Often the extended family of grandparents, parents, aunts, uncles, and cousins would gather around the piano and sing favorites, like "Amazing Grace," as well as all the carols at Christmas time. How proud I felt when I was asked to play the piano for these hymn-singings.

On family vacations we sang hymns to make the miles pass by more quickly. I especially loved to hear my father's deep baritone voice singing "There is a Balm in Gilead." My mother claimed she couldn't carry a tune, but she knew the words to most of the hymns in *The Baptist Hymnal.* And so did I. To pass the time on one of our long trips, my mother, my sister, and I once had a hymn-quoting contest. My ability to recite from memory all stanzas to a large number of hymns made me the winner.

In my religious tradition hymn-singing played a prominent role in worship. Sometimes the portion of the service consisting of three or four hymns was called the "song service." As a child, I saw the worship service divided into two distinct parts: singing and preaching (and there was no doubt which I liked best!). It was fun to stand and sing to the top of my voice, to feel the words and the rhythms, to be part of a mighty chorus of praise to the Creator.

When I was old enough to sit quietly through the sermon, my parents let me join my older sister on the second row of the church. We were still under the watchful eyes of my mother, who sat several rows back, and my father, the preacher at the front who could see

all. I was around seven years old, and my sister Anne was ten. By this time I could read the words to the hymns we sang, whether or not I understood all their meanings.

A hymn frequently sung in our church was "Break Thou the Bread of Life." Every time we came to the last line of the first stanza, Anne and I doubled over to keep from laughing out loud. When we got home, we could restrain ourselves no longer. Over and over again we sang the line, "My spirit pants for Thee, O living Word," laughing so hard that tears ran down our cheeks. Our parents' explanation of the meaning of the line made no difference. To us, we were singing about our underpants.

It is natural for children to interpret language according to their own experience. In creative ritual we all recover our childlike playfulness and spontaneity. Including the experience of all is vitally important to the participation of everyone. Because hymns engage our senses and emotions as well as our intellects, the words of hymns become embedded in us at the conscious and subconscious levels.

Hymns play a powerful role in ritual experience. Through the blending of rhyme and meter, sound and meaning, hymns shape our beliefs and actions. The words we sing are important. Singing praises to "Father," "Master," "Lord," and "King" helps form and support dominant-submissive systems. These images take root in the literal imaginations of children, shaping their concepts of themselves and the Divine as they develop into adults. (For this reason I have gathered inclusive songs, stories, and prayers especially for children in my book *God, A Word for Girls and Boys.*)

My own experience leads me to believe that "adult" hymns also influence the faith development of children, as well as adults. The hymns in *Praying with Christ-Sophia* invite people of all ages to full participation in sacred experience. I began writing these hymns when I had grown to the awareness of my feelings of exclusion when singing traditional hymns. First, I tried to change all the masculine language, and then I found myself unable to sing the songs I had loved so long. The music that was part of my being carried words that brought pain instead of nourishment to my spirit.

One Christmas, the multitude of masculine images in traditional carols felt like stones pelted at me, bruising my spirit. I decided to try writing some new words to familiar Christmas carol tunes. My first text came quickly and joyfully: "O Come, Christ-Sophia" to the tune of "O Come, All Ye Faithful." My younger son and I tried it out to his guitar accompaniment, feeling together the fun of creation. The next week I wrote "Christ-Sophia Now We Praise" to the tune of "Hark, the Herald Angels Sing."

I took these new hymns to our local clergy-women's meeting. Hearing the enthusiastic voices of these women and seeing the excitement on their faces convinced me that my hymn-writing was a holy calling. Although these women had received the official blessing of their churches through ordination, several told me after the meeting that singing hymns inclusive of the divine feminine gave them a deeper feeling of value than they had ever experienced.

In the following months the hymns kept coming—more than I had anticipated and with greater energy than I had ever experienced in my writing. Sometimes a line or two would come to me at unexpected times and places. I might be driving to work and have to pull over to the side of the road to jot down a stanza. Several times I dreamed lines to hymns. Often I worked out the rhymes and meters as I was exercising on the Stairmaster.

My joy increased as I took these hymns to my worship community called New Wineskins. (The name comes from Matthew 9:17.) These women and a few men received my hymns with such eagerness and delight that I felt inspired to develop other ritual resources and to collect them all into this book. The encouragement and affirmation of the New Wineskins Community helped bring this book to birth.

Growing out of my experiences of pain and joy, the hymns in this collection have a prominent place. The music is included with the hymn texts for ease of use. The services in this collection suggest hymns to be included. The hymns also stand separately so that they can be used with other services and in settings other than formal worship services.

Ultimately, my hope is that singing the hymns in this collection—either alone or together with your own worship community—will deepen your experience of the sacred Presence.

Using this Book in Communities

The services here are designed for a variety of communities. After years of being excluded and devalued by traditional male-dominated rituals, women may experience the most immediate healing and renewal through these services. The inclusion of the divine feminine in worship can help women for the first time feel that sense of affirmation and power that men have experienced for centuries through masculine images of God.

Men are slowly beginning to realize the importance of a gender-balanced sacred symbolism for themselves as well. They may begin by embracing inclusive ritual as an ethical issue, as a way of contributing to justice for women. But through ritual experience in community, they come to feel the importance of including the divine feminine for their own emotional and spiritual well-being. They find freedom to move beyond stereotypes of masculinity and femininity to develop their full humanity.

The services in this collection are thus intended not only for communities of women but also for communities inclusive of women and men of various races and ages. Some services, like those celebrating Thanksgiving and Earth Day, specifically invite intergenerational participation. Other services focus more on adult experience, but can be adapted to include children. The main purpose of this book is to encourage creative participation, not to provide forms to be followed rigidly. The individual needs of each community and the creative gifts of the members should guide the use of these services.

A theological principle at the foundation of this collection is that all people are created in the divine image and thus have equal value. These services are created for communities that practice a radical equality, communities in which all are pastors and priests to one another.

All the services are built on the participation of everyone. The rituals take place with participants gathered in a circle, a physical symbol of the principle of equality. One or several persons will need to take responsibility for planning and implementing each service. But this responsibility should be rotated among members of the community, so that no one person becomes the leader. All should be encouraged to exercise freely and creatively their unique gifts.

Using this Book for Individual Meditation

Individuals, as well as communities, can use the services in this book. The prayers, litanies, and stories may stimulate personal meditation. Individuals can use parts of services that invite participants to share feelings with the community as starting points for journal entries. For example, in the "Celebration of Independence Day," participants are invited to take turns placing on the altar symbols of areas in their lives in which they are striving for freedom and symbols of areas in their lives in which they experience freedom. Individuals can gather these symbols for private reflection and write about feelings of pain and victory in their struggle for freedom. In the "Celebration of All Saints' Day," participants are invited to bring pictures of persons they consider to be saints and to talk briefly about these saints. As a part of personal meditation, an individual can reflect in writing about a saintly person.

The hymns in this collection may be sung by individuals as well as by communities. One of the members of the New Wineskins Community said she wanted to memorize "We Sound a Call to Freedom" (sung to the tune of "Mine Eyes Have Seen the Glory") so that she could sing it when she was driving to work or at other times when she needed to feel empowered. Individuals can also read the hymns aloud or silently as poems for prayer and meditation.

This collection comes to you as an invitation to join the creative adventure of developing egalitarian sacred symbols and rituals that bring healing and power to all living beings. It is my prayer that both communities and individuals will find healing and renewed power through *Praying with Christ-Sophia*.

A note about the text: The services in this book often use Scripture passages for the prayers and communal responses. In many of these, I have inserted "Christ-Sophia" where "Christ" alone originally appears.

SERVICES

CELEBRATION OF BEGINNINGS

This service can take place any time of the year. It can be used to celebrate the beginning of a new faith community or as a celebration of beginnings for individual members, such as beginning a new school year, beginning a job, beginning a relationship, beginning a project, beginning a degree program, or beginning retirement from a job.

Before the service, ask persons who are beginning something new to bring a symbol of whatever they are beginning. If this service is celebrating the beginning of a new faith community, ask members to bring symbols of their feelings about this beginning. Gather either indoors or outdoors, depending on the season of the year. Sit in a circle around an altar. On the altar place a mustard seed and yeast (dry or caked).

Longing for Beginning

Group 1   We long to begin again.
We hunger for the fresh word.
We thirst for the new experience.

Group 2   We come to this community because we long for the new.
Old words no longer speak to our spirits.
Old forms cannot contain our voices.

Group 1   This community of Christ-Sophia offers new beginnings.
Christ-Sophia invites us to begin a new kind of community,
a community of equals,
a community of justice,
a community of creative spiritual growth.

Group 2   We have begun this community;
we are beginning this community;
we shall begin this community.

Group 1   This is a community of continual beginnings.
Each gathering is a beginning.
Each connection is an opening to new wisdom from Christ-Sophia.

Group 2   Christ-Sophia continually inspires our beginnings.
We cannot rest on past revelations.
We long for the new.

All   Gracious Christ-Sophia, hear our longings.
Come with us on our journey into the new.
Inspire us as we begin. Amen.

Resistance to Beginning

Voice 1 Why are you always wanting to begin something new? Just when I've begun to adjust to the last change, you want to start something else.

Voice 2 I would like to begin with you, but I want to know more about where we are going. You can't expect me to go blindly into something. I want to see a well-developed plan first.

Voice 3 My trouble is just getting started. Every time I want to start a new project, the hardest part is beginning. Even though I may feel excited about the project, I just can't get started. I sabotage my project by letting everything get in the way.

Voice 4 Does that sound familiar! I love to write, but beginning is always agony. That blank page or blank computer screen stares at me, and I freeze. It seems as though I get up and down a hundred times before I begin. I go get a drink of water, arrange my desk, straighten everything in the house—anything to keep from beginning.

Voice 5 All of you are so creative. I feel so dull. Sometimes I'd like to start a creative project, but I've never been creative. I can't write or draw or decorate. A teacher once praised a poem I wrote, but I believe she was just trying to make me feel good. I don't know what to begin.

Voice 6 I've been wanting to start graduate school, but I'm afraid I might not be smart enough. Even though I've done well in all my academic work, I'm always afraid I might fail. If I begin a graduate degree and something comes up that keeps me from finishing it, I will feel like a failure. My parents taught me to finish everything I start.

Voice 7 When I was in high school, I tried out for a leading part in a play. I was so excited to get the part. My parents were so proud of me and invited all of our relatives to the performance. At a crucial place in the performance, I forgot my lines and had to be prompted. I felt so embarrassed and ashamed.

Voice 8 I won't ever begin another art project. My last show got mediocre reviews, and I felt ashamed and angry. If my work is not appreciated, why should I even bother?

Voice 9 Coming to this community was a real beginning for me. It's quite a stretch for me to sing and pray to Christ-Sophia. Can't we settle down for a while and not start anything else?

Hymn of Challenge "Stir Us Out of Our Safe Nest, Mother Eagle," #30

Meditation on Beginning

As one member of the group reads the following meditation out loud, the others meditate silently.

Beginning a race, starting an essay, beginning a community—beginning anything—stirs up many feelings within us. We feel excited as we anticipate something new; perhaps we are restless to get started. But at the same time we feel afraid to take that first step, anxious about the unknown. Maybe we're not sure we have all it takes to finish the project, so we wonder if we should even start.

Beginning is the process of bringing something new into being. Through beginning we become cocreators with the One who, in the beginning, created the universe. Through beginning we become connected with the origin of all things.

Beginning takes faith: faith in ourselves and faith in our connection with the Creator. Believing that the Source of all things is at work within us, we can overcome our fear and begin. No matter how small the first step or timid our beginning, the very act of beginning something new is powerful.

Jesus told two parables, found in Luke 13:18–21, that illustrate the power of small, insignificant beginnings. A farmer sowed a mustard seed in his field (*take the mustard seed from the altar and hold it up*). Even though the mustard seed is the smallest of all seeds, it grew and became a tree, and the birds of the air made nests in its branches. Who would ever think that this tiny seed could become a large tree?

A woman took a little yeast and mixed it with more than a bushel of flour (*take the yeast from the altar and hold it up*). Silently, invisibly, the yeast spread throughout the whole mass, until it had risen. Then she baked it, and it became a delicious loaf of bread. Who would ever think that savory, fresh-baked bread began as this small, smelly substance? Jesus illustrates divine reign through these two parables of amazing possibility in even the smallest, most insignificant, even invisible beginnings.

Beginning something new is a sacred act. It is an act of seeking the Creator within and embracing our own creative gifts. Beginning is a covenant with the one who began all creation. Beginning is an expression of hope in the future. Beginning is a commitment to new life. "Whatever you think you can do or believe you can do, begin it. Action has magic, grace, and power in it" (Goethe).

Affirmation of Beginnings

Those who have brought symbols of things they are beginning come to the altar one by one, place their symbols on the altar, and talk about their feelings as they begin. If this service is celebrating the beginning of a new faith community, members can bring to the altar symbols of their feelings about this beginning. After each one finishes, the whole community gives the following affirmation:

> We celebrate your beginning;
>> we rejoice in your courage to claim your gifts.
> May you feel your connection with the great Creator
>> as you begin your creative adventure.
> May you feel Christ-Sophia walking with you,
>> giving you wisdom and power for each new step.

Visualizing Beginnings

Each member finds a comfortable place to sit or lie down. One member reads the following guided meditation.

Close your eyes. Now begin taking deep breaths. Breathe in...and breathe out...deeply...and slowly. Breathe in deeply and slowly through your nose...breathe out slowly through your mouth. Breathing in...and breathing out...slowly...and deeply, feel the breath of the Spirit flowing through your whole body and soul. Breathe in slowly and deeply through your nose...breathe out slowly through your mouth. Continue breathing in...and breathing out...slowly and deeply, knowing that you are breathing the Spirit.

As you continue breathing in...and breathing out...slowly and deeply, let your imagination see yourself as you are beginning your new adventure. See yourself moving with confidence and grace as you begin. What are you wearing?

See yourself in your favorite colors walking into your new place, claiming your new space.

Feel your skin tingling with excitement, while you continue breathing deeply...and slowly... feeling completely at peace with yourself and the world as you breathe slowly...and deeply the breath of the creative Spirit.

Look around you. What do you see? What do you smell? What do you hear? Relish each new sight and sound and smell, as you feel more alive than before. As you continue breathing the breath of the Spirit, slowly breathing in...and breathing out, you feel peaceful and powerful, confident to move into the new challenge. Filled with the breath of the creative Spirit, as you breathe in...and breathe out...slowly and deeply, you begin.

Now come back to this community, open your eyes, and feel again the support of one another as you look forward to beginning.

Hymn of Celebration   "Celebrate a New Day Dawning," #1

Healing Ritual

If possible, choose a season of the year and a place that allows movement from indoors to outdoors. Begin in a home or meeting room. Sit in a circle around an altar. On the altar place vessels containing baby oil or body lotion, vessels containing burning incense, a pot of herbal tea, and cups for each participant.

Lamenting Abuse

Women   Birthgiver, who gave us life in all its fullness,
        who created us in your own image,
        look at us now!
We came forth full,
        and now we are empty;
        you have dealt harshly with us;
        you have brought calamity upon us.
Call us no more "blessed,"
        for we have lost your original blessing.
Call us "bitter,"
        for you have dealt bitterly with us (Ruth 1:20–21).

Our bodies, born in beauty and wholeness,
        have been misused and harassed,
        sometimes subtly and insidiously,
        other times openly and blatantly.
Battered and raped, we have cried
        out for help.
And we have heard,
"This can't happen in my church";
"Such a good member of my church wouldn't do that";
"A good, faithful wife stays with her husband
        and prays that he will change";
"Don't dwell on your abuse, just forgive and forget";
"If you pray and have enough faith, everything will be all right."

Our minds, born to reason and think,
        have been called irrational and weak,
        incapable of making important decisions
        in the church and in the world.
Our spirits, born to love and create,
        have been stifled and ridiculed,
        devalued and labeled unworthy
        of handling sacred rituals.

When we express deep feelings,
    we hear voices of scorn, taunting,
"Isn't that just like a woman!"
When we create,
    we hear voices of ridicule, saying,
"That's too soft and sentimental!"
When we enjoy our bodies,
    we hear voices of judgment, saying,
"She's just asking for it!"

How long will you hide your face from us,
    Christ-Sophia, our hope and our strength?
We come seeking your face,
    knowing that you fully understand
    and share our deepest suffering.
For you too have been stifled, abused, and scorned.
When you lived on earth in our brother Jesus,
    you were misunderstood and crucified.
Your Spirit lived on but in distorted form.
Your feminine face has too long been ignored and denounced,
    and we have not known you, sister Sophia.
Christ-Sophia, we ask not that you rescue us,
    but that you empower us to connect with your Spirit within us.
Then together we will rise from abuse
    to wholeness of life,
Together we will become the glorious,
    joy-filled creation you intended.
Then, once more, we will be blessed.

Men   Almighty God, you created us fully in your image,
    and we are supposed to be mighty like you,
    or so we've been taught
    through word and song and images and actions
    in church and everywhere we turn.
You are "He,"
    and we are "he,"
    so we must act like "he-men."

When we do not act like men are supposed to act,
    we are scorned as "sissy," "pansy," "wimp."
If we do not play rough and tough,
    we hear voices of ridicule, taunting,
"You play like a girl!"
When we have cried,
    we have been told,
"Boys don't cry!"

When we have painted pictures and cared for children,
   we have heard,
"Men can't make enough money doing that!"
We are expected to fix tires and leaky faucets and the world,
   and we are tired and sick.

The abuse we suffer most often goes unnoticed,
   for we abuse others with our dominance and power.
Our bodies, created in beauty and strength,
   have suffered violence of war and of competition.
Being dominant forces us to be forever vigilant,
   so that no one takes away our power.
Our minds, created to reason,
   have too often been consumed with irrational anger,
   when we lose some of our territory.
Our spirits, created for love and joy,
   have been stifled with fear and greed.
Our hearts suffer anguish as
   the terrors of death surround us.
We see violence and strife all around us
   and cringe from the violence we find within us.
O that we had wings like doves to fly away from
   the "macho" man image that surrounds us and
   threatens our survival (Psalm 55:4–6).

Come and save us, O gentle Spirit!
For it was you who took us from the womb
   and kept us safe on our mother's breast (Psalm 22:9).
You gave us birth,
   and you are still there for us.
Come near to us,
   for we need your help.
You are *El Shaddai*,
   not only "God almighty"
   but also "the breasted God."
You are not only "he,"
   but also "she."
We need your strength and your tenderness
   so that we can be all you created us to be,
   strong in our gentleness,
   and gentle in our power,
   giving up dominance and privilege for the deeper privilege
   of living in mutual love and peace and harmony
   with all creation.

All   Creator of all the little children of the world,

red, brown, yellow, black and white,
   are we really precious in your sight?
We are the little ones;
   do we really belong?
We are weak,
   but are you strong?
Why do you leave us alone
   when we hurt and cry?
Where are you when we
   call for help?
Can you hear us?
Can you help us?
Our fathers get angry
   and yell at us and hurt us;
Our mothers shut their ears
   to our cries for help;
We have been taught to call you
   "Our Father."
Are you like our fathers?
Can we call you "Our Mother?"
Would you be any better to us then?
Who are you anyway,
   and do you really care about us,
   your little ones?
We want to sing and laugh and dance,
   but how can we,
   when we feel so bad?
What have we done wrong?

Lover of little ones, come and help us,
   for we don't know what to do.
It's not our fault
   that our fathers and mothers hurt us.
We are small and weak,
   but you understand,
   because you were once a child.
Holy Child, our sister and brother,
   take us with you to a land
   where we can run free and unafraid,
Where we can laugh and play
   all day long with you.

One woman Earthmaker, you created me
   in fullness and delight,
   with rare beauty and rich goodness.
I am Earth, your marvelous creation.

What has become of me?
I have been raped and scraped,
    used and abused
    in the service of profit and greed.
The human creatures think my treasures are theirs
    to use for their own gain.
They cut down my forests,
    strip greenness from my land,
    kill my animal friends,
Fill my oceans and air
    with deadly waste.

When I cry out for help,
    they proudly respond,
"God gave us dominion over you!"
Their religions teach them to conquer,
    not to nurture me.
How long must I suffer this abuse?
How long can I survive?
Can they not see that their own survival
    is also at stake?

My Maker, help them to see that
    I am yours,
    not theirs.
The wild animals of the forest are yours;
    the cattle on a thousand hills are yours;
    all the birds of the air are yours;
The mountains and the oceans are yours;
    the trees and the fields are yours;
I am yours,
    and all that is in me is yours (Psalm 50:10–11).

Spirit within me and within every living being,
    fill their hearts with reverence for me.
May they see their close connection with me
    so that they will give up dominion
    and live in partnership with me,
    restoring my rare beauty and rich goodness.

Cries for Healing

Reader 1   We have all suffered abuse. Growing up in patriarchal religions and cultures, we have been devalued, demeaned, stifled, and ignored.

Women	Women have suffered abuse. We have been physically, emotionally, and spiritually raped. Our sacred power has been denied; our creative energies have been stifled. Our femininity has been devalued. Our gifts have been scorned; we have been labeled "witches" and "bitches." We cry out for healing.
Men	Men have suffered abuse. Patriarchal religion and culture, though exalting maleness, have also taken their toll on us. We have been programmed to be tough and strong. Having to control society and ourselves has been too big a burden to bear, causing us to die young. Our emotions have been stifled. Our feelings have dried up. Our creativity has waned. We cry out for healing.
Reader 2	We live in a society which rapes the earth, scorns the feminine, and worships the masculine. By denying deity a female face, we deny the value of the feminine in ourselves and in all creation.
All	We all suffer from this spiritual abuse. Our bodies, minds, and spirits feel the wounds of long abuse. We all cry out for healing. How long, how long must we wait? When will our healing come?
Reader 3	Our healing comes as we recover from years of abuse by reclaiming our innate spirituality. Healing comes as we open ourselves to new revelations of deity that will help us revalue women, men, and all creation.
All	Sacred symbols give deepest value. Our healing will come as we value the divine feminine and the divine masculine through our sacred symbols. We have a long way to go, but we can wait no longer. We must begin the journey toward recovery. We cry out for healing now!

Hymn of Healing   "Come, Christ-Sophia, Healing Power," #5

Words of Healing

Reader 1	I say to God, my rock, "Why have you forgotten me? Why must I walk about mournfully because the enemy oppresses me?" As with a deadly wound in my body, my adversaries taunt me, while they say to me continually, "Where is your God?" (Psalm 42:9–10)
Reader 2	Can a woman forget her nursing child, or show no compassion for the child of her womb? Even these may forget, yet I will not forget you (Isaiah 49:15).
Reader 3	I am poured out like water, and all my bones are out of joint; my heart is

like wax; it is melted within my breast; my mouth is dried up like a potsherd, and my tongue sticks to my jaws; you lay me in the dust of death (Psalm 22:14–15).

Reader 4   As a mother comforts her child, so I will comfort you; you shall be comforted in Jerusalem (Isaiah 66:13).

Reader 5   Why do you hide your face? Why do you forget our affliction and oppression? For we sink down to the dust; our bodies cling to the ground (Psalm 44:24–25).

Reader 6   Happy are those who find Wisdom and those who get understanding, for her income is better than silver, and her revenue better than gold. She is more precious than jewels, and nothing you desire can compare with her. Long life is in her right hand; and in her left hand are riches and honor. Her ways are ways of pleasantness, and all her paths are peace. She is a tree of life to those who lay hold of her; those who hold her fast are called happy. Wisdom will be a healing for your flesh and a refreshment for your body (Proverbs 3:8, 13–18).

Reader 7   You keep my eyelids from closing; I am so troubled that I cannot speak. I consider the days of old, and remember the years of long ago. I commune with my heart in the night; I meditate and search my spirit (Psalm 77:4–6).

Reader 8   Jesus says, "Come to me, all you that are weary and are carrying heavy burdens, and I will give you rest. Take my yoke upon you, and learn from me; for I am gentle and humble in heart, and you will find rest for your souls." Come to Sophia to receive instruction and give your shoulder to her yoke, for in the end you will find rest in her (Matthew 11:28–29; Sirach 6:25,28; 51:26).

Invitation to Healing (in unison)

Christ-Sophia calls us to come and be healed, saying,
    "Come to me! Come to me!
    There is life in my words and healing in my touch."

Hymn of Invitation   "Do You Want to Be Healed," #10

Healing Touch

Move in procession outside to a large open space surrounded by lush vegetation, if possible. Participants carry the vessels containing baby oil or body lotion, the vessels containing burning incense, the pot of herbal tea, and the cups; place them on an altar (some kind of table or stones and boards). All sit, on chairs or on the ground, in a circle around the altar. Place one chair in front of the altar.

Participants take turns sitting in the chair in front of the altar, making a brief statement of their specific need for healing or, if preferred, a general statement of desire for healing. Others come forward, take oil or lotion from the altar, pour it in their hands, and anoint the person for healing. (Use hands and oil or lotion in a way that feels comfortable to participants, such as massaging shoulders, hands, head, and/or feet.) As they are applying healing touch, participants speak one of the following sentences or other healing words of their choice:

> In the name of Christ-Sophia, claim your healing.
>
> Arise daughter (son), and be set free from all that binds you.
>
> Be healed of all that prevents your wholeness.
>
> Feel the healing Spirit touching your body and making you well.
>
> Be healed, in the name of Christ-Sophia.

Breathing in Healing

Stand about five feet apart. One person stands in the center to lead this guided meditation, reading the following words:

Close your eyes, and begin taking deep breaths. Breathe deeply and slowly in and out…raising your arms straight up over your head, breathe in deeply through your nose. Breathe out slowly through your mouth as you lower your arms back to your side. Raise your arms and move them in a wide circle over your head as you slowly inhale. Complete the circle as you lower your arms and slowly exhale. As you continue this movement, visualize a healing light entering your head and moving throughout your body…breathing in…breathing out…feel the healing light flowing through your body…from head to foot.

Breathe in the healing power of Christ-Sophia…breathe in the healing wisdom of Christ-Sophia. Breathe out all that limits the healing power within you. Breathe in…and breathe out. Breathe in peace…breathe out fear…breathe in healing…breathe out disease. Feel the deep love and wisdom of Christ-Sophia flowing through every cell of your body, bringing peace and healing.

Cup your hands at your side, palms up, and slowly move them up your body as you breathe in, slowly and deeply. Breathe out slowly as your circle your hands over your head and lower them back to your side. Continue this movement, visualizing warm moisture from the earth flowing up from your feet through every cell of your body…breathing in…breathing out…feel the healing warmth flowing through your body…from the soles of your feet to the crown of your head…flowing upward…healing…reviving…empowering.

Breathe in the healing warmth of our Sister-Brother Earth…source of energy flowing throughout your body-soul…breathing in… breathing out…hands moving and circling with your healing breath. Healing peace…healing love…healing power flows freely through your body-soul. Breathe in the Spirit that flows through all creation, now freely flowing through you as you breathe in…and breathe out. Feel the healing power of Christ-Sophia. Feel the healing warmth of Sister-Brother Earth freely flowing through your whole body-soul.

Drinking in Healing

Participants sit in the chairs (or on the ground) in a circle around the altar. One person gives a cup from the altar to each person and then takes the teapot and pours the herbal tea into the cup of the person on his or her left. That person then takes the teapot and pours tea for the person on her or his left, and so on around the circle until everyone has a cup of tea. Participants lift their cups over their heads while reading the following blessing.

Reader 1   Drink the healing tea from our Sister-Brother Earth.

Reader 2   Drink with gratitude for the healing gifts of our Sister-Brother Earth.

Reader 3   Drink the life-giving power of Christ-Sophia.

Reader 4   Drink the cup of Sister-Brother Earth.

Reader 5   Drink in the healing love of Christ-Sophia.

Reader 6   Drink in the healing peace of Christ-Sophia.

Reader 7   Drink in the healing warmth of Sister-Brother Earth.

All   We drink the cup of Sister-Brother Earth.
We drink the healing power of Christ-Sophia.
We claim our full healing.
We celebrate the divine feminine and the divine masculine
   in each of us and in all creation.
We celebrate our sacredness.
We claim our holy power.

Closing Hymn   "Rise Up, O People, Proclaim Christ-Sophia Has Risen," #27; stanza 2 only

BLESSING RITUAL

Gather outside, if weather permits, on Sunday morning or another time considered by the community to be the most sacred in the week. Sit in a circle around an altar. On the altar place a ministerial stole (hand-woven if possible), fresh flowers (one for each participant) candles (one for each participant), and a box of matches. Beside the altar place a kneeling cushion or bench.

Invocation of Blessing *(in unison)*

> Creator of all life, you blessed us when you gave birth to us. You called us "good," and you opened a world of possibilities to us. But somewhere along the way we lost the assurance of your original blessing. Other voices stifled your voice of blessing within us, and we doubted our worth. Our rituals have given us the feeling that some are more blessed than others, that some are your specially chosen ones, that some are called by you for a special purpose and others are not. Today we come to reclaim your blessing upon us all and to affirm your call in our lives. Come to us, Spirit from whom all blessings flow. Restore and awaken us with your deepest blessing. Amen.

Doxology *(in unison, sing or speak stanza 1 of "Come, Thou from Whom All Blessings Flow," #8)*

> Come, thou from whom all blessings flow;
> Wake us to see more than we know;
> Help us claim all our gifts and pow'r;
> Fill us with grace that we may flow'r. Amen.

Longing for Blessing

One of the participants reads the following story to the others.

Once there were twin unicorns named Damion and Daphne. Bright and beautiful they were as they laughed and played in the forest. They delighted the other forest animals with their singing and prancing and telling of stories. Daphne and Damion were so much alike that they often knew what the other was thinking. They loved each other dearly and loved being together.

Damion and Daphne early learned to worship the Great Maker of unicorns and of all creation. They learned that the Maker had given them unique abilities to increase love and beauty throughout the world. The

Ministers of the Great Maker instructed the twins in all the ways of worship, devotion, and service. They admonished Daphne and Damion over and over, "Let nothing and no one stand in the way of your allegiance to the Great Maker. Listen closely for the call of the Maker. And above all else, go wherever the Maker leads. No task is too hard, and no burden is too great when you follow the Maker."

As they grew, Damion and Daphne became more devoted to the Great Maker and more attentive to the words of the Ministers. They pondered all they heard and listened carefully for the call of the Maker. They decided to go apart from each other for a little while so that they could listen more attentively for the Maker's call. They went their separate ways, deep into the forest to fast and listen for their call.

Several days later Daphne and Damion came together again. With a new strength and confidence in her voice, Daphne began, "I have heard the call of the Maker. My call is to be a Minister of the Maker."

Damion hesitated, "But…but, is that possible? Is that…is that…permissible? I wonder if that will be allowed."

Daphne responded with even greater confidence, "Why, of course, it is possible. The Maker has called me. How could there be any objection? The Ministers have taught me that above all else, I should follow where the Maker leads."

"Of course, of course, oh, of course! How wonderful!" Damion, beginning softly, was now shouting for all the forest to hear. "Of course, you should follow the call of the Maker. Nothing will stand in your way! It thrills me to hear of your call, for I too have heard the call of the Great Maker. My call is also to be a Minister of the Maker."

Together, Daphne and Damion pranced and sang and danced their praise to the Great Maker. Other forest animals gathered round them in curiosity. Some peered from behind the trees, and others came right up to Daphne and Damion to ask the cause of their jubilation.

"We have heard the call of the Great Maker!" Damion exclaimed. "And we look forward to following the call!"

"Then we must set aside a Feast Day for you to announce your call to the assembly and to receive the blessing of the Ministers," said an older unicorn.

All the inhabitants of the forest eagerly anticipated the next great Feast Day. For at that time the two brightest young unicorns in the forest would reveal their visions from the Great Maker. In preparation, Daphne and Damion fasted and prayed and praised the Maker. The other animals scurried round the

assembly hall, shining and polishing and arranging until everything was in perfect order. Others sweated over huge stoves to prepare the sumptuous feast that would follow the ceremony.

On the morning of the Feast Day animals came from all parts of the forest to the great assembly hall. A hushed expectancy filled the hall as they waited for Damion and Daphne to enter. First, the sable-robed Ministers of the Maker entered. Closely following them came Daphne and Damion, more radiant than ever before.

The Chief Minister stepped up to the High Place and addressed the assembly: "All creatures, great and small, formed by the hand of the Great Maker, hear me this day. We have gathered together to bless two of our number who have heard the call of the Maker. We want to stand with them as they pledge to do as the Maker has directed. First, we will hear Damion's call and bless him, and then Daphne."

Trembling before the large assembly, Damion began, "I am called to be a Minister of the Great Maker." That was all he needed to say. The minute the words were out of his mouth, shouts of praise thundered throughout the hall. "Hallelujah! Blessed be the Great Maker who has called one of our sons as Minister! Blessings on Damion who has chosen to follow the Maker in this highest of callings!" These cries of blessing went on for what seemed hours.

Finally the Chief Minister silenced the crowd and said: "Blessings upon you, Brother Damion, for letting nothing stand in the way of your allegiance to the Great Maker. Remember that no task is too hard, and no burden is too great when you follow the Maker's call. Now we will perform the ceremony of anointing."

Hundreds of Ministers of the Maker from many forests filed by and solemnly anointed Damion. Placing a large, glowing purple ring on Damion's horn, the Chief Minister declared: "From henceforth, Damion the unicorn, you are an official Minister of the Great Maker. You have all the duties and privileges of this high calling, including standing in the High Place and performing the most sacred rites."

Now it was Daphne's turn. Full of joy and faith from the blessing Damion had received, Daphne stepped forward and announced, "I too am called to be a Minister of the Great Maker." She paused expectantly, but heard only Damion's voice and a few other voices affirming, "Praise to the Maker who has called one of our daughters as Minister. Blessings on Daphne who has chosen to follow the Maker in this calling." Others stared in disbelief. Others looked confused. Undaunted, Daphne repeated, "I am called to be a Minister of the Great Maker."

A heavy silence followed. Then the Chief Minister rose to his full height and addressed the assembly: "There seems to be some misunderstanding here. We all know how important it is to follow the call of the Maker. But this call comes in many forms. The Maker does not call she-animals to be Ministers. Daphne must be mistaken about her call. Now, of course, she-animals can be called to minister in many capacities, but they cannot be Ministers of the Maker. And they can never be anointed to stand in the High Place and to perform the most sacred rites. This is just not meant; this is not meant at all. Our Sacred Writings say that only he-animals can be Ministers. Do you want to restate your call, Daphne?"

Feeling shocked and betrayed, Daphne hung her head and said softly, "All I know is that I heard the Maker call me to be a Minister. And you taught me the importance of following this call. But you also taught me to trust the Ministers and what you say about the Sacred Writings. So I guess I must find ways to minister without being a Minister."

Throughout the next few years Daphne searched for what it would mean for her to minister without being a Minister of the Maker. But no matter what she did, she could not silence the soft, persistent voice of the Maker:

"You are to be my Minister. I have equipped you to be my Minister. Go forth and follow my call."

Perplexed, Daphne went to the Chief Minister and said, "I have tried to minister without being a Minister of the Maker, but I cannot find peace. I keep hearing the call of the Maker to be a Minister. And you have always taught that following the Maker's call is most important of all."

In his most august tone, the Chief replied, "That is not what I meant. That is not what I meant at all."

Deferentially, Daphne questioned, "What then did you mean?"

"Well, you see, the Maker has created," he began, shifting anxiously, "you see, the Maker has created he-animals for certain tasks and she-animals for other tasks. And she-animals were not created to be Ministers of the Maker. Thus say the Sacred Writings. You must have misunderstood the Great Maker."

Daphne left feeling even more bewildered. But still she worked, and still she loved, and still she searched for ways to minister without being a Minister. Her brother, Damion the Minister, offered words of comfort and reassurance, "One day they will understand."

Daphne heard voices full of pain, deep within the forest crying out for help. And she went to them. Even though she was not an official Minister, she could not stay away from the hurt ones. She listened to their cries, and she prayed for healing. But some asked, "Are you an anointed Minister of the Maker?"

Daphne would have to answer, "I am called to minister even though I am not an anointed Minister." Some would then turn away and refuse the healing.

But still Daphne worked, and still she loved, and still she searched for the deep meaning. One day the voice of the Maker was unmistakable: "Daphne, the unicorn, I have called you to be my Minister."

"But. . . but," she stammered, "Is that possible? Is that permissible? The Chief Minister says that the Sacred Writings prohibit she-animals from being Ministers."

"Do you not know that it was I who gave the Sacred Writings? Would I ask you to do something that is prohibited in my Writings? The Chief Minister and many others have misinterpreted the Sacred Writings. Search the Sacred Writings for yourself."

Daphne studied the Sacred Writings for herself. Just as she had originally thought, before the Chief Minister had put doubts in her mind, the Sacred Writings told of she-Ministers, as well as he-Ministers. Throughout the Sacred Writings, she read about the sacred value of she-animals and he-animals and about the Maker's calling she-animals and he-animals to be Ministers.

Daphne went before the Ministers and told them of her discoveries in the Sacred Writings. But they frowned and said, "That is not what they mean. That is not what they mean at all."

With unshakable resolve, Daphne replied, "I have heard the call of the Maker over and over again. And I have studied the Sacred Writings and found that she-animals can be Ministers of the Maker. I will no longer turn my back on my call. I can no longer let anything or any animal stand in the way of my allegiance to the Great Maker. I must go wherever the Maker leads and do whatever the Maker says. No task is too hard, and no burden is too heavy when I follow my Maker. With or without your blessing I must follow the call of the Maker. I will be a Minister of the Maker."

That day Daphne did not receive the blessing of the Ministers. But she received the greater blessing of the Maker, and she became a Minister of the Maker. She healed with great power and love and joy. And she taught and preached the sacred value of all animals—she and he.

Placing a large, glowing purple ring on Daphne's horn, her brother, Minister Damion, declared: "Daphne, you are a Minister of the Maker. One day they will understand."

Invite all present to tell their stories of longing for blessing or of receiving blessing.

Hymn of Hope   "Hope of Glory, Living In Us," #13

Blessings from Scripture

Reader 1   But now in Christ-Sophia you who once were far off have been brought near. For Christ-Sophia is our peace; Christ-Sophia has broken down the dividing wall, that is, the hostility between us (Ephesians 2:13–14).

Reader 2   For as in one body we have many members, and not all the members have the same function, so we, who are many, are one body in Christ-Sophia, and individually we are members one of another. We have gifts that differ according to the grace given us: prophecy, in proportion to faith; ministry, in ministering; the teacher, in teaching; the exhorter, in exhortation; the giver, in generosity; the leader, in diligence; the compassionate, in cheerfulness (Romans 12:4–8).

Reader 3   For just as the body is one and has many members, and all the members of the body, though many, are one body, so it is with Christ-Sophia. For in the one Spirit we were all baptized into one body—Jews or Greeks, slaves or free—and we were all made to drink of one Spirit. Indeed, the body does not consist of one member but of many. If the foot would say, "Because I am not a hand, I do not belong to the body," that would not make it any less a part of the body. And if the ear would say, "Because I am not an eye, I do not belong to the body," that would not make it any less a part of the body.

As it is, there are many members, yet one body. The eye cannot say to the hand, "I have no need of you," nor again the head to the feet, "I have no need of you." Now you are the body of Christ-Sophia and individually members of it (1 Corinthians 12:12–16, 20–21, 27).

Reader 4   There is no longer Jew or Greek, there is no longer slave or free, there is no longer male and female; for all of you are one in Christ-Sophia (Galatians 3:28).

Reader 5   You are all part of a chosen race, a royal priesthood, a holy nation, God's own people, in order that you may proclaim the mighty acts of Christ-Sophia who called you into marvelous light (1 Peter 2:9).

Reader 6   I will pour out my Spirit upon all flesh, and your sons and your daughters shall prophesy (Acts 2:17).

Reader 7   You are the light of the world. A city built on a hill cannot be hid. No one after lighting a lamp puts it under the bushel basket, but on the lampstand, and it gives light to all in the house (Matthew 5:14–15).

Experience of Blessing

Participants take turns putting on the ministerial stole and kneeling on the cushion or bench beside the altar, making a brief statement of their specific calling. The others pass by, laying hands on the person's shoulders and/or head and softly speaking words of blessing. After each person has been ordained, she or he takes a flower and a candle from the altar. After the last person has received ordination, she or he strikes a match and lights the candle of the person to his or her right. That person does the same, and so on around the circle until all candles are lighted.

Communal Affirmation of Blessing

Reader 1   Christ-Sophia has broken down the walls that separate men and women, ordained and unordained.

All   We have all been ordained by the Spirit who lives in this Body of Christ-Sophia, and we are truly blessed. We are the light of the world. Christ-Sophia calls us to give light to new visions:

Reader 3   Visions of wholeness and unity;

Reader 4	Visions of the breaking down of all walls that keep us from becoming all God created us to be;
Reader 5	Visions of all gifts being nurtured and celebrated and expressed within the Body of Christ-Sophia.
Men	In the vision, the men will not say to the women, "I have no need of you."
Women	And the women will not say to the men, "I have no need of you."
All	One age group will not say to another age group, "I have no need of you." One race will not say to another race, "I have no need of you." Instead we will recognize our need for one another and for mutuality in all relationships.
Reader 6	For there is no longer Jew or Greek, there is no longer slave or free, there is no longer male or female; for we are all one in Christ-Sophia (Galatians 3:28).
All	We have put on Christ (Galatians 3:27); we have embraced Wisdom (Proverbs 4:8); we now incarnate Christ-Sophia. We are called and ordained to make the vision reality, to fulfill the mission of "making all things new" (Revelation 21:5).

Hymn of Blessing and Challenge   "Send Us Forth, O Christ-Sophia," #28

Parting Blessing (*stand and speak in unison*)
> We have felt the deepest blessing of Christ-Sophia
> > through this community of faith.
> We go forth with the blessing reverberating
> > through our whole beings,
> > empowering us to fulfill our mission.
> As we part, we affirm
> > the fullest ordination of the Spirit
> > upon each one of us:
> Inspiring us to claim
> > our gifts and calling;
> Challenging us to make our visions plain
> > for all to see and celebrate.
> Now may we depart
> > in peace and hope and power,
> > knowing we are indeed blessed,
> > now and always.

PEACEMAKING RITUAL

Gather in a circle either indoors or outdoors. In the center of the circle create an altar with symbols of peace, such as doves and peace pipes and olive branches. Also on the altar, place paper, pencils, a large ceramic bowl, and matches. Close to the altar place two collages: one with images of things that impede peacemaking, and one with images of things that contribute to peacemaking.

Invoking the Spirit of Peace (*in unison*)

> Spirit of Peace,
> > who dwells within us and inspires us
> > with visions of the way the world should be,
> Heighten our awareness of your presence
> > as we gather here this day.
> May we learn to follow Christ-Sophia,
> > who models peace through partnership
> > and teaches us all the things
> > that make for peace, now and always.

Exorcising Things that Impede Peace

As individuals speak, they hold up the collage with images of things that impede peacemaking. As each voice speaks, several other voices chant softly, "No peace, no peace."

Voice 1	Approximately 14.9 million American children, one in five, live in poverty.[7]
All	There can be no peace until such poverty is eliminated. Poverty impedes peace. Depart, demon of poverty.
Voice 2	Over half a billion men, women, and children in the world suffer from hunger.[8]
All	There can be no peace until such suffering is eliminated. Hunger impedes peace. Depart, demon of hunger.
Voice 3	In the United States, every eleven days a woman is murdered by her husband or boyfriend, and every fifteen seconds a woman is battered by a man.[9]
All	There can be no peace until such violence is eliminated. Violence breeds violence. Depart, demon of domestic violence.

Voice 4	One in four American girls will have been sexually assaulted by the age of eighteen; millions of children around the world are forced into prostitution and other forms of slave labor.[10]
All	There can be no peace until such abuse is eliminated. Abuse breeds abuse and violence. Depart, demon of child abuse.
Voice 5	Seventy percent of the world's poor are women; 66% of women's work is unpaid.[11]
All	There can be no peace until such injustice is eliminated. Discrimination against women impedes peace. Depart, demon of gender injustice.
Voice 6	People all over the world experience violence and discrimination because of their sexual orientation.
All	There can be no peace until such discrimination is eliminated. Prejudice based on sexual orientation impedes peace. Depart, demon of heterosexism.
Voice 7	A scant 13% of U.S. congressional leaders are minorities; only about 11% of U.S. congressional leaders are women.[12]
All	There can be no peace until such inequities are eliminated. Prejudice against racial minorities and women of all races impedes peace. Depart, demon of institutional racism and sexism.
Voice 8	Religious institutions are dominated by white men. Traditional religious language and imagery sanction the dominance of white men.
All	There can be no peace until such dominance is eliminated. Patriarchy impedes peace. Depart, demon of patriarchy.

Participants mention other things that they believe impede peacemaking. After each speaks, the whole group responds with "Depart, demon of_____."

The Challenge to Peacemaking

Reader 1	They have treated the wound of my people carelessly, saying, "peace, peace," when there is no peace (Jeremiah 6:14).
Reader 2	If you, even you, had only recognized on this day the things that make for peace! But now they are hidden from your eyes (Luke 19:42).
All	We look for peace, but find no good, for a time of healing, but there is terror instead (Jeremiah 8:15).

Reader 3   Deceit is in the mind of those who plan evil, but those who counsel peace have joy (Proverbs 12:20).

Reader 4   Depart from evil, and do good; seek peace, and pursue it (Psalm 34:14).

All   Let us then pursue what makes for peace and for mutual upbuilding (Romans 14:19).

Reader 5   These are the things that you shall do: Speak the truth to one another, render in your gates judgments that are true and make for peace (Zechariah 8:16).

Reader 6   Happy are those who find wisdom, and those who get understanding, for her income is better than silver, and her revenue better than gold. Her ways are ways of pleasantness, and all her paths are peace (Proverbs 3:13–14, 17).

All   And a harvest of righteousness is sown in peace for those who make peace (James 3:18).

Hymn of Challenge   "Let Justice Like Waters Roll Down on our Land," #14

Celebrating Things that Contribute to Peace

As individuals speak, they hold up the collage with images of things that contribute to peace-making. As each voice speaks, several other voices chant softly, "Make peace, make peace."

Voice 1   Habitat for Humanity helps eliminate poverty around the world by helping poorly sheltered families build homes for themselves and their communities.

All   Habitat for Humanity makes peace in our world. Decent housing contributes to justice and peace. Blessed be the peacemaking work of Habitat for Humanity.

Voice 2   United Nations Children's Fund saves millions of lives of children all over the world through increasing the rate of immunization.

All   United Nations Children's Fund makes peace in our world. Saving children's lives contributes to justice and peace. Blessed be the peacemaking work of UNICEF.

Voice 3   Volunteer high school and university students help disadvantaged people in our country and around the world to become self-supporting.

All	Volunteer students make peace in our world. Helping disadvantaged people contributes to justice and peace. Blessed be the work of volunteer students.
Voice 4	United States citizens advocate for hungry people all over the world through organizations like Bread for the World and Seeds of Hope.
All	Concerned citizens use the democratic process to make peace. Advocating for hungry people contributes to justice and peace. Blessed be the peacemaking work of advocacy groups.
Voice 5	Women's shelters help break the cycle of domestic violence through advocacy and counseling services for victims and their families, and through emergency shelter and legal aid.
All	Women's shelters make peace in our world. Eliminating domestic violence contributes to peace. Blessed be the peacemaking work of women's shelters.
Voice 6	Congregations around the world observe children's sabbath to celebrate the gift of children, to seek justice for children, and to help protect children from all forms of abuse.
All	Congregations observing children's sabbath make peace. Seeking justice and protection for children contributes to peace. Blessed be the peacemaking work of these congregations.
Voice 7	Many human rights organizations lobby against discrimination based on sexual orientation and promote AIDS prevention, treatment, and research.
All	Human rights organizations make peace in our world. Advocating against sexual discrimination contributes to peace. Blessed be the peacemaking work of human rights organizations.
Voice 8	United Nations World Conferences on Women promote women's rights to safety, education, and health care, and help women achieve equal access to economic and political power.
All	United Nations World Conferences on Women make peace. Promoting justice for women contributes to peace. Blessed be the peacemaking work of women's conferences.
Voice 9	Inclusive worship communities challenge patriarchal religion that denies equality because of skin color, culture, gender, class, age, disability, and sexual preference.
All	Inclusive worship communities make peace in our world. Freeing reli-

gion from patriarchy contributes to justice and peace. Blessed be the peacemaking work of inclusive communities.

Participants mention other things that they believe contribute to peacemaking. After each speaks, the whole group responds with "Blessed be the peacemaking work of _____."

The Blessings of Peace

Reader 1   Blessed are the peacemakers, for they will be called children of God (Matthew 5:9).

Reader 2   Steadfast love and faithfulness will meet; righteousness and peace will kiss each other (Psalm 85:10).

All   The fruit of the Spirit is love, joy, peace, patience, kindness, generosity, faithfulness, gentleness, and self-control (Galatians 5:22).

Reader 3   The effect of righteousness will be peace, and the result of righteousness, quietness and trust forever (Isaiah 32:17).

Reader 4   For you shall go out in joy, and be led back in peace; the mountains and the hills before you shall burst into song, and all the trees of the field shall clap their hands (Isaiah 55:12).

All   By the tender mercy of our God, the dawn from on high will break upon us, to give light to those who sit in darkness and in the shadow of death, to guide our feet into the way of peace (Luke 1:78–79).

Reader 5   As shoes for your feet put on whatever will make you ready to proclaim the gospel of peace (Ephesians 6:15).

Reader 6   And let the peace of Christ-Sophia rule in your hearts, to which indeed you were called in the one body (Colossians 3:15).

All   Christ-Sophia is our peace; Christ-Sophia has broken down the dividing wall, that is, the hostility between us (Ephesians 2:14).

Song of Peace   "O Come Join Hands, All Violence Cease," #20

Peace Offerings

Participants take paper and pencils from the altar and write down commitments or contributions they will make to peace. Then they fold their papers and place them in the ceramic bowl on the altar. One person lights a match and burns the papers, while the whole community speaks the following response in unison:

Spirit of Peace,
 we make these covenants with you,
 knowing that they are inspired by you.
Inflame our spirits with passion and power
 to keep these peacemaking covenants.
Give us new visions of a peaceful world
 and of the ways our contributions
 can help to make this world a reality. Amen.

Visualizing Peace

Each participant finds a comfortable place to sit or lie down, while one person reads the following guided meditation.

Close your eyes and begin taking slow, deep breaths. Inhale slowly, counting to eight. Exhale slowly, counting to eight. Breathe in deeply and slowly through your nose...and breathe out slowly through your mouth. Breathe in deeply, filling your whole body-soul with the spirit of peace...breathe out slowly, letting go of all that blocks peace in your life...breathing in...and breathing out...slowly...and deeply, feel the spirit of peace within you and surrounding you.

As you continue breathing in...and breathing out...slowly...and deeply...and peacefully, imagine yourself fulfilling the covenant of peacemaking you just made. What are you doing? See yourself making your contribution to peace. Where are you? Look around you and notice sights and sounds and smells. Imagine your feelings as you make your contribution to peace. Imagine the response you desire from others.

As you continue breathing in...and breathing out...slowly...and deeply, imagine the difference you make with your contribution to peace. Visualize what you want to happen when you make your contribution to peace. What change do you want to happen? Visualize this change taking place, just as you desire in the depths of your spirit.

As you slowly come back to this community and open your eyes, continue to see yourself changing the world through your peacemaking work.

Passing the Peace

Go around the circle exchanging words of peace, such as the following:

May the peace of Christ-Sophia go with you,
 filling you with joy and hope
 in believing that you have power
 to make your visions of peace reality.

RENEWAL OF HOPE & POWER FOR CHANGE

Before this service, ask participants to bring to the community a symbol of something they are working to change. Some may prefer to bring a poem or a brief story describing this work. If possible, choose a season of the year and a place that allows movement from indoors to outdoors. Pick a colorful outdoor place, filled with trees and flowers.

Begin in a small, dimly lit room. At the front of the room place an altar filled with traditional religious symbols. Sit in rows facing the altar. As participants arrive, play traditional hymns.

A Parable

One person reads the following parable to the community.

Once there was a woman who lived in a prison. But she did not know it was a prison, because she had never seen anything else. She was born in this prison, and this is where she had grown up. She went to school in this prison and made many friends there. Her family lived in this prison also. They had never seen anything else.

Although the rooms in the prison were small and dark, they felt safe and secure. Work here often felt confining and boring, but there were times for games. While some games were not allowed, others were encouraged. And everyone knew the rules.

The woman had held a variety of jobs in the prison. She had taught the children the rules of the games. She had helped people who were having trouble adjusting to the conditions in the prison. And she performed some of the sacred rituals that kept people feeling safe and secure. She spent many hours studying sacred texts so that she could perform these rituals correctly.

One day as she was studying, she found a book on the history of the prison. In the book she learned that there once was a time before the prison existed. The book also told about places outside the prison. She couldn't believe

this because no one had ever told her about these places, and she had never seen anything else when she looked outside the windows. The book pointed her to a window through which she might be able to see something beyond.

The woman went to the window and looked out. At first the light that struck her eyes was so bright that she could see nothing else. She started to turn away from such a bright light for fear she might be blinded. But curiosity kept her gazing through the window. Gradually her eyes adjusted to the unfamiliar light, and she began to see colors unlike anything she had ever imagined—brilliant splashes of gold and purple and rose. She felt drawn toward these colors by a distant, almost-forgotten longing in her soul. All of a sudden she felt her spirit would burst if she had to stay inside another moment. Her heart racing, barely able to catch her breath, she began running around the room, hands moving along the walls, searching for a way out.

Finally she came to a crack in the wall. With all her might she pushed against that crack. Feeling a slight movement, she pushed again and again and again. At last she gathered all her strength and threw her whole body against the crack in the wall.

The crack opened just enough for her to squeeze her aching, bruised body through. She found herself in a dark corridor facing a small door with a rusty doorknob. She turned and pushed and pulled on the doorknob, but it would not budge. She kept on turning and pulling the knob while she pushed against the door. Finally, gathering up all her strength and will, she opened the door.

On the other side, she could not believe the sights and sounds around her. Forgetting the pain of her struggle, she began dancing and swaying as the wind blew through her hair, singing a song she had never even heard. Laughing and skipping through fields of rich purple and green, her spirit felt free and alive and creative. Her delight sprang forth in songs and poetry; her joy grew with the flowers she planted along her path. How could she have lived so long not knowing such a world of beauty and freedom existed? She came to a lush green meadow and lay down to rest, basking in the sunlight. At last she had found her true home. Exhausted, but deeply satisfied, she fell asleep.

In a dream she heard a voice. At first the voice was just a whisper, but then it grew louder and louder. The voice said, "I am your sister Sophia. You have found a place of light and freedom beyond what you have ever seen or felt before. This is your true home. But you cannot rest here. You must go back to the prison and bring others here."

When the woman awoke from her dream, she knew what she must do. Reluctantly and sadly, she walked back toward the prison. She knew that Sister Sophia was right. She could not fully enjoy her newfound freedom and delight while those she loved were still in prison.

Back in the prison, she began to tell others about life outside. Some laughed and called her crazy, saying, "Why haven't we ever heard about this place outside? If there were such a place, we would have read about it in our sacred texts." The woman tried to tell them that it was there in the texts all along.

Many believed, and she pointed the way to the door behind the crack in the wall. They too had to work hard to open the door. Some gave up, preferring the comfort and security of the prison to this difficult struggle toward an unknown future. But some persisted until they opened the door to the world outside where they too saw visions and sang songs they had never known.

Feeling encouraged, the woman went back to the prison to tell others. In her role as leader of sacred rituals, she believed she could move people toward the light outside. So she began to change the rituals and sacred symbols to reflect the light and freedom outside the prison. Again some laughed, but others raged: "How dare you change our sacred rituals? These have been good enough for centuries! Who gave you the power to change things? If you keep this up, we will take away your job as leader of rituals."

Undaunted, she met with others who had seen the light outside the prison. Together they wrote new interpretations of the sacred texts, sweeping away the dust of centuries of tradition to let the light shine through. In their rituals they celebrated their new experiences, often taking excursions outside the prison to drink deeply the breath of freedom. But the voice of Sophia within always beckoned them to go back to lead others toward the light.

Voices of caution counseled the woman to be careful when she went back inside. The prison could be a cruel and dangerous place. People she loved advised her to speak softly and walk carefully, watching where she stepped. If she didn't watch out, she could destroy not only herself, but others whom she loved. The prison keepers might see them connected with her in the effort to lead people out of the prison.

Discouraged and saddened, she went outside where she could catch her breath and lie down in the lush green meadow. How could she keep from speaking the truth and revealing the beauty she had discovered? How could she be cautious when the light blazed in her soul? She wanted to shout through every room in the prison the way to freedom. She had grown tired of going back and forth between the prison and the world outside. Longing to stay outside, she wanted to break open the prison doors and release all the prisoners. If she kept going back into the prison, her spirit might not get the fresh air it needed to survive. If she kept stifling her spirit, it might die.

Exhausted and deeply burdened, she fell asleep. In a dream, she heard a voice. This time she knew the tender, strong voice of her sister Sophia: "Fear not. Your spirit will never die. Your spirit is my spirit within you. I understand your pain. For I too have been stifled—for centuries. Your mission is a holy mission, for you are resurrecting me. Claim my wisdom to choose carefully when to speak and when to be silent. When you are silent, you do not stifle your spirit. You simply choose to share your spirit with those who are willing to open their eyes to the light.

"My sister, together we will choose carefully the times and places to share our spirit. Together we will find the faith and peace to live in between the prison and the light. Arise in the power of our spirit, confident that we are opening prison doors so that one day all will walk freely into the light."

The woman awoke, refreshed with wisdom and hope and courage to live in between.

Hymn of Hope   "Come to Me, All You With Heavy Hearts," #9

Struggling Toward Change

Participants take turns coming to the altar with their symbols of the change they are working toward. Each replaces one of the traditional symbols on the altar with her/his symbol of change and then gives a brief interpretation of the symbol. Those who brought a poem or story will take a traditional symbol off the altar before reading. After each one finishes, the community responds with the following words:

> May you feel the power of Christ-Sophia,
>   dwelling within you,
>   filling you with abundant hope
>   for your holy work of change.

Hymn of Challenge   "Holy Christ-Sophia," #12

Process outdoors while singing; then sit or stand in a circle.

The Witness of the Tulip Tree

One person reads the following poem while the others meditate.

> In late winter,
>   when the grass is still
>   yellow and brittle,
>   a bloom appears overnight
>   on a bare branch.

One bloom is quickly joined by another
    and another until the whole tree
    radiates peach-pink warmth
    through the coldness.

The tulip blooms stand full and perfect
    on their branches,
    like china cups lined neatly
    on wooden shelves.
Blossoming on the verge of spring,
    the tulip tree promises beauty to come.

As quickly as they appear,
    the tulip blossoms disappear
    from the tree, like dew evaporating
    in the morning light.
In their place spring green leaves
    and greenness everywhere.

And so it is with Christ-Sophia
    in the world today,
    blossoming on the edge of awakening,
    a sign of beauty and wholeness.

Whenever we see the vision in full bloom,
    standing pink and proud
    in a cold, barren land,
Our hearts quicken with hope
    of the lush greenness
    that will soon cover the whole earth.

Hymn of Invitation   "Welcome Our Sister-Brother Creator," #35

Closing Call to Change   (based on Matthew 9:17; Revelation 21:5)

Voice 1   New wine cannot be contained in old wineskins.

Voice 2   The skins will burst, and the wine will be spilled.

Voice 3   New wine must be put in new wineskins.

All   We have drunk the new wine of Christ-Sophia, and we cannot be con-
                  tained in old structures and old symbols. Old language will not suffice.
                  Old rituals do not satisfy. Our vision can be stifled no longer. We cannot
                  wait for official authorization or approval.

Voices of Resistance	*(two, in unison)* Have patience. Change takes time. Move slowly. Be careful; be cautious.
All	We cannot be contained. We can wait no longer. Our message is too urgent. Our gifts are too precious. Our vision is too compelling. New visions become new realities. New realities create new expressions.
Voices of Affirmation	*(two, in unison)* Proclaim the vision of Christ-Sophia. Dance the vision. Sing the vision. Write the vision. Teach the vision. Preach the vision. Paint the vision. Live the vision.
All	Christ-Sophia calls us to live the vision of justice, peace, and mutual relationships. Mutual relationships create new forms and symbols.
Voices of Resistance	*(two, in unison)* People just aren't ready. Give them more time. Don't make waves. Don't be so pushy. You're overreacting. You're making a big deal over a few little words.
All	We are new wine, and we cannot be contained. We are bursting out of old language and old rituals.
Voices of Resistance	*(three, in unison, growing louder)* Be careful! You might lose your job. You might split the church. Go along; get along; fit in. Be patient; be cautious; be sweet. BE QUIET!
All (*loudly*)	WE CANNOT BE SILENT! WE CANNOT BE CONTAINED! WE ARE BURSTING OUT OF THE OLD! WE ARE CREATING THE NEW! WE EMBODY CHRIST-SOPHIA, WHO SAID, "SEE, I AM MAKING ALL THINGS NEW!"

LITURGY FOR WISE AGING

Before this service, ask participants who feel that they are aging to bring two symbolic objects: one symbolizing what they are leaving behind, and the other symbolizing what they are gaining as they move on. These people should be self-selected, instead of designated according to some chronological age.

As the group gathers, play classical music. Form two circles, one inside the other. Those who feel they are aging sit in the inside circle. The others sit in the outside circle. Place a table in the center to serve as an altar. On the altar place a paper sack, small pots containing potting soil, a bowl containing seeds, and a pitcher of water.

Hymn of Invocation   "Come, Christ-Sophia, Our Way," #6

Meditation on Aging
One person in the group reads the following meditation aloud.

Music, art, and literature that have stood the test of time are called "classics." We put the highest value on wine that has aged. But people who have stood the test of time are not called "classics." We put little value on aging people. We give them such labels as "hags," "little old ladies," "old codgers," "geezers," and "dried-up raisins."

Our society worships at the altar of youth. In movies and on television and in magazines, beauty comes in the form of youth. Our culture places highest value on youth. We equate romance with youth. Businesses and institutions desire youthful leaders. Fearing loss of beauty and romance and power, we desperately try to hang on to youth by dyeing our hair, having plastic surgery, going on grueling exercise and diet programs.

By our language and our actions we demean aging people. We devalue their ability to make meaningful contributions to society. Some cultures look to older people for wise counsel, but we shuffle them aside. By ignoring the gifts and graces of our elders, we are all diminished. We cannot become all we

are created to be until we place sacred value on life at every age.

Biblical revelation places great value on aging people. In ancient Israel those who held positions of authority were "elders." These older members of the community performed important tasks of local government and justice (Numbers 11:16–30). In the early Christian community the leaders were elders, serving as decision-makers and ministers (Acts 15:6-21; 1 Peter 5:5; James 5:14). Scripture equates aging with Wisdom (*Sophia* in Greek), a personification of deity. Sophia gives age sacred value. Sophia is older than the earth. Wisdom says, "Ages ago I was set up, at the first, before the beginning of the earth" (Proverbs 8:23). Wisdom is old. Old people have wisdom.

Our aging leads toward wisdom when we place high value on ourselves as we change and grow. As we age wisely, we leave some things behind. We may need to grieve some losses. But wise aging also means that we move toward new experience with hope and eagerness. We can then celebrate what we gain as we age.

Litany of Mourning (all stand)

Inner Circle   An uncertain future lies ahead as we age. We fear the unknown. We fear the losses we may suffer.

Outer Circle   We hear your fear and anxiety. Standing with you, we go with you into the future. We feel with you the fear of the unknown.

Inner Circle   We join together to mourn our losses. Connecting with one another, we share our pain. We grieve for what is no more.

Outer Circle   We hear your pain. Standing with you, we join in your sorrow. We grieve with you for what is no more.

Inner Circle   Our youth is no more. We mourn the loss of our youth.

Outer Circle   We want to understand what your losses mean to you. Help us understand so that we may feel with you.

All sit down again. The people in the inner circle take turns sharing their symbols of what they are leaving behind. They reflect on feelings of regret and loss. A person in the outer circle takes the paper sack from the altar and hands it to a person in the inner circle. This person places her or his symbol in the sack and passes it to the others in the group who do the same. Then the person takes the sack out of the room.

Litany of Celebration (all stand)

Inner Circle   Our worth does not lie in our youth. We are much more than our youth. The certainty of youth was only an illusion.

Outer Circle   Your value does not depend upon your youth. Our value does not depend upon our youth. We are all much more than our youth.

Inner Circle   We feel hope as we move on. Claiming power to reject demeaning labels, we call ourselves wise elders and classics.

Outer Circle   We feel your hope and power. You are wise elders and classics. You have much wisdom to give to us all.

Inner Circle   We gain wisdom as we age. Embracing the gifts of each moment, we discover new meaning and new creativity.

Outer Circle   We value your growing wisdom, and desire to learn from you. We celebrate your new discoveries.

Inner Circle   Though we have suffered loss, we celebrate gains as we move on.

Outer Circle   We want to celebrate with you. Help us understand what you are gaining.

All sit down again. The people in the inner circle take turns sharing their symbols of what they are gaining as they move on in life. They reflect on their feelings of hope, and share dreams for the future. Then they place their symbols on the altar in the center of the circle.

As members of the group read the following passages, the others meditate upon the passages and upon the symbols on the altar.

Scriptural Affirmations of Aging

Reader 1   The righteous flourish like the palm tree,
    and grow like a cedar in Lebanon.
They are planted in the house of God;
    they flourish in the courts of our God.
In old age they still produce fruit;
    they are always green and full of sap (Psalm 92:12–14).

Reader 2   Wisdom was set up, at the first, before the beginning of the earth. Wisdom took part in establishing the heavens and the foundations of the earth (Proverbs 8:23, 27, 29).

Reader 3   Within Wisdom is a spirit
    intelligent, holy, unique, manifold,
    subtle, active, incisive, unsullied,
    lucid, invulnerable benevolent, sharp,
    irresistible, beneficent, loving,
    steadfast, dependable, unperturbed,
    almighty, all-surveying,
    penetrating all intelligent, pure
    and most subtle spirits.
For Wisdom is quicker to move than any motion;
    she is so pure, she pervades
    and permeates all things (Wisdom 7:22–24).

Reader 4   Wisdom deploys her strength from one end of the earth to the other, ordering all things for good. Wisdom makes all things new (Wisdom 8:1; 7:27).

Reader 5   Let your souls receive instruction from Wisdom. For in the end you will find rest in her (Sirach 51:26; 6:28).

Reader 6   I will pour out my Spirit upon all flesh,
    and your sons and your daughters shall prophesy,
    and your young people shall see visions,
    and your old people shall dream dreams (Acts 2:17).

Hymn of Celebration   "We Claim Your Support, Christ-Sophia, Our Rock," #32

Take the small pots containing potting soil from the altar, and give one to each person in the inner circle. Pass the bowl of seeds around the circle. Each person takes a few seeds and plants them in the pot while telling the group what dream or talent or hope she or he would like to see blossom in her or his life.

The people in the outer circle then pass around the pitcher of water, each one pouring a few drops of water on the seeds of each person in the inner circle. The people in the inner circle place the pots back on the altar. All stand and form one big circle, while praying the following benediction.

Benediction *(in unison)*

> Send us forth Sophia, our Wisdom, with new dreams and bright visions. Even as we mourn what we have left behind, we celebrate all we are moving toward. Divine Wisdom, may we see in you the sacred value of age. Open our eyes to discover new meaning and creativity as we age wisely and well in your image. Empower us to let go of the old and embrace the new as we continue to blossom into all you created us to be. Amen.

Turn the classical music back on and pass around glasses of aged wine, continuing the celebration of all that has stood the test of time.

NURTURING CREATIVITY

Gather in a circle outdoors, if the weather is temperate. Choose a place with lush vegetation of varied colors. In the center of the circle, place an altar. Leave a space in the center of the altar. Around this space, place paper of different colors, magic markers, colored chalk, finger paints, pens, play dough, and musical instruments. Place a large trash can near the altar. As participants arrive, play meditative music.

Lament Over Stifled Creativity

Group 1   Loving Birth-giver, Holy Ruah, you brought us into this world full of joy and wonder and possibility. Your laughter filled our souls as we ran freely, like children, through fields of splendor, feasting our eyes on bluebonnets iridescent in spring sunlight, drinking in smells of sweet honeysuckle, singing with the meadowlarks, rolling down hills of fresh mowed grass.

Group 2   But somewhere along the way we lost our senses. Instead of "Try it," we heard, "Stop! Be Careful!" We have been molded and shaped into neat boxes by those too fearful of the free spirit in us and in themselves.

Group 1   O Creative Spirit, some of your children have been stifled and squeezed almost to the point of destroying your life within them. Broken by violence and abuse and neglect, they cry out, and we cry with them.

Group 2   But they have survived, and so have we! We are all on the path to recovery from abuse of our creative souls.

All   Our spirits, though weakened, live on.
Our childlike wonder, though stifled, lies deep within us.
Our creative powers, though buried, can rise again
   to new life and freedom.
O risen Christ-Sophia, bring our creativity back to life.
Inspire us with your playful energy.
Guide us with your wisdom.
Fill us with your overflowing beauty, now and always. Amen.

Two Voices

One person reads this dialogue aloud.

Creating is so much fun! I have a whole day free to create. I'll get up early and start. I can't wait to see what I'll create! I know I'll make something beautiful and unique.

Just who are you fooling? Do you remember the last day you set aside for your creative work? You didn't even begin until you had cleaned the house and paid the bills. You talk about how much you love creating, but I think you avoid it.

Order nurtures my creativity. I believe the creative process involves bringing order out of chaos. So I begin by straightening and cleaning, creating order in my external environment. Then I feel freer to move on in my creative work.

Sounds like an excuse to me! You waste so much time that you could be spending on your real creative work. And anytime you come to the least little snag, you get up and walk around the house and look out the windows, or go outside for a walk.

My creative spirit loves the beauty of nature. Looking out at the trees and squirrels or going for a walk in the woods nourishes my creativity. Surrounding myself with greenness gives me energy. When the flow slows down or stops, I know I need to feed my soul with beauty.

With all the time you spend straightening and taking breaks, you have little time left for your creative work. You produce so little in a day. How much do you have to show for your last full day of creativity?

What matters to me is not how much I produce, but whether I follow the playful, Creative Spirit of Sophia within me. The final product is not so important as the fun of the process.

Sounds like another excuse to me. With your busy schedule and all the pressures of your job and the constant cacophony of life in the city, I don't know why you even bother with creativity. Seems like a luxury to me. The free days you have aren't enough to produce anything of any consequence. You might as well give up.

I think of creativity as a way of life, not just an activity for isolated parts of my life. Creativity is always happening in my subconscious if not my conscious mind. Then when I have the chance to give it expression, I try to clear away distractions. Even the distraction of your voice!

But I am here to remind you of your insignificance, lest you get a "big head" about what you're doing. Your work is not really that creative. Your ideas are trite and silly.

It makes me angry to hear you say that! My creative work is important and beautiful. But sometimes I fear that people won't appreciate it. I'm afraid that my work is either too late or too soon or not good enough. Then I realize that pleasing my creative spirit brings satisfaction whether or not others approve.

Sounds like another rationalization to me. You're afraid your creative work won't get the recognition you know it deserves. And you're afraid that your creative flow will dry up.

Leave me alone! Voice of judgment and fear and distraction and anger, I will not listen to you another minute. Voice of the Creative Spirit of Sophia, speak forth your inspiration and encouragement! From now on I will follow your voice.

Rising up out of deepest blue ocean,
   Sophia smiles her invitation.
Her dark, dancing eyes
   beckon me to come to her
   as she waves an ostrich feather toward me.
Carefree and careful,
   her sonorous voice soothes my fear,
   like a cello calming the timpani.
She calls me to move
   out toward fullness.
Lavishly laughing,
   she swims closer.
I wade cautiously out,
   and she smiles her delight.
Finally I plunge in,
   beyond the confines of conventionality.
Swimming out to meet her,
   I take the feather
   from her outstretched hand.
The feather becomes my quill
   and the ocean, my ink—
   an unending flow.

Hymn of Encouragement   "Tread Lightly on Your Heavy Path," #31

Participants go to the altar and choose materials to create symbols of what stifles their creativity and symbols of what nurtures their creativity. Participants may choose to draw or paint their symbols, to write poetry or prose, to develop music or drama. Encourage playful, spontaneous activity. Allow about fifteen minutes for this creative work. Play soft music, according to the community's preference, during this time. Participants take turns sharing their symbols of stifled creativity. After doing so, they throw them in the trash can. After all have finished, the community responds with the following affirmation:

We are all in the image
of the Creative Spirit.
Our creative work is too precious to stifle.
Our creativity is sacred,
and we will allow nothing to stifle it.

Participants take turns sharing their symbols of nurtured creativity. After doing so, they place them in the center of the altar. After all have finished, the community responds with the following affirmation:

There is nothing more valuable
than our creative gifts.
Our creativity is worth
the most sacred nurture.
Led by the Creative Spirit within us,
we will nurture our creativity.

The Call of Holy Beauty
One person reads the following poem while the others meditate.

Holy Beauty beckons through our rush of motion and noise,
whispering through the gentle spring breeze,
calling us to stop and notice.

Divine Beauty shouts through flaming rose sunsets,
singing through purple and yellow fields of glistening wildflowers,
and we still do not notice.

Beauty shines and sings through all creation,
for those with eyes to see the holiness in every blade of grass,
and ears to hear the music in the smallest insect's voice.

Static may interrupt and threaten to overwhelm,
but the music overcomes,
and the truth plays on in purest strains.

Thoughtless hands may mar and scar,
but the splendor shines through,
and the freshness blooms again.

Holy Beauty calls us to join her in giving birth,
to come alive to the creative spirit within us,
to bring forth beauty in all we touch.

Holy Beauty calls us to notice, to nurture,
to claim the fullness of our creative power,
to cocreate with her a world beyond imagining.

Hymn of Invitation and Benediction   "Come, Holy Beauty," #7

LITURGY FOR MOURNING LOSS

Before the service, ask participants to bring two symbols of a loss they are mourning: one symbol of some memory they want to hold on to, and one symbol of some memory they want to let go of. These may be pictures or anything that represents the loss. The loss may be of a relationship through death, divorce, or separation necessitated by abuse. It may be the loss of some physical ability through illness or accident. It may be the loss of place that comes with a move, the loss of a house, or something else that holds meaning. It may be the loss of a job or of some dream.

If possible, choose a season of the year and a place that allows movement from indoors to out-doors. Begin in a dimly lit room, sitting in a circle around an altar. On the altar place one large candle in a holder, matches, a ceramic bowl, a small shovel, and small candles to equal the num-ber of participants. As the service begins, light the large candle.

Call to Mourning *(one member reads)*

> We come together today to share the pain of loss. Our hearts ache with grief. Our tears pour out the pain that lies deeper than words. We cry out in our woundedness. We long for relief from the unrelenting stabs of grief. Is there any help? Can we find comfort?

Feelings of Grief

Voice 1
> Grief feels like a lump of dough—heavy, gooey, and raw,
>> sitting in the pit of my stomach, never going away.

Voice 2
> Grief feels like an elephant sitting on my chest,
>> heavy and pressing down,
>> keeping me from taking a deep breath.

Voice 3
> Grief feels like a vast, salty sea,
>> flowing from my eyes in never-ending tears.

Voice 4
> Grief feels like falling into a dark hole,
>> falling deeper and deeper,
>> wondering if I'll ever get to the bottom.

Voice 5
> Grief feels like a cold night without a jacket,
>> a long way from home.

Voice 6
> Grief feels like ants crawling through my insides,
>> stinging in tender places.

Voice 7   Grief feels like a long nightmare,
            from which I struggle to wake up, but can't.

Voice 8   Grief feels like fear—fear that it will never end,
            fear that it will end and then what?

Cries of Lament

Reader 1   Call me no longer Naomi (pleasant),
            call me Mara (bitter),
                for the Almighty has dealt bitterly with me.
            I went away full,
                but God has brought me back empty (Ruth 1:20–21).

Reader 2   For my sighing comes like my bread,
                and my groanings are poured out like water.
            Truly the thing that I fear comes upon me,
                and what I dread befalls me.
            I am not at ease, nor am I quiet;
                I have no rest; but trouble comes...
            Therefore I will not restrain my mouth;
                I will speak in the anguish of my spirit;
                I will complain in the bitterness of my soul (Job 3:24–26; 7:11).

Reader 3   I am utterly bowed down and prostrate;
                all day long I go around mourning.
            For my loins are filled with burning,
                and there is no soundness in my flesh.
            I am utterly spent and crushed;
                I groan because of the tumult of my heart (Psalm 38:6–8).

Reader 4   By the rivers of Babylon—
                there we sat down and there we wept
                when we remembered Zion.
            On the willows there
                we hung up our harps (Psalm 137:1–2).

Reader 5   Oh, that I were as in the months of old,
                as in the days when God watched over me...
            When I was in my prime,
                when the friendship of God was upon my tent;
                when the Almighty was still with me,
                when my children were around me;
                when my steps were washed with milk,
                and the rock poured out for me streams of oil! (Job 29:2, 4–6)

Struggling with Grief

Group 1   We know grieving our losses is normal and healthy,
        but sometimes we feel that we are going crazy,
        that things will never be the same.

Group 2   Things can't ever be the same;
        our losses can never be replaced.
    People tell us we can marry again,
        have another child,
        find a new relationship.
    But we know we can't replace our lost loves.

Group 1   Sometimes we even grieve the loss of unhealthy relationships.
     We grieve for what never was;
        we grieve for lost dreams,
        for lost fantasies of perfect intimacy.

Group 2   Even when we choose to let go, we still grieve.
    We cry for the lost relationship or job,
        although we chose to let go for our own well-being.

Group 1   Grief does not move in a steady, straight line
        from stage to stage, from beginning to end.

Group 2   Grief circles in and out of pain and numbness,
        guilt and anger,
    Spiraling up and down, moving toward acceptance.

Group 1   Acceptance does not come overnight or on cue.
    We let go slowly and cautiously,
        fearing the emptiness.
    Even grief is something to hold onto.

Group 2   The struggle of grief is the struggle to let go,
        the struggle to let go of what we have known.
    Whether or not we have chosen the loss,
        we still struggle to let go.
    Can we hold on to some memories?

Holding on to Memories

Participants take turns going to the altar with their symbols of memories they want to hold onto. Each talks briefly about his or her symbol, then lights a small candle from the large candle on the altar, and returns with the candle and the symbol to the circle. After each one finishes, the whole community gives the following response:

Hold fast to your good memory,
   letting it bring you warmth and light
   as you walk your path of grief.
We will walk with you,
   sharing your memory
   and accepting your pain.
Through our connection with one another,
   we feel the Spirit of all comfort.

After everyone is finished, give hugs to one another and then do a group hug.

Letting Go of Memories

Participants move outside, taking the ceramic bowl, matches, shovel, and their symbols of memories they want to let go of. Depending on the place and the desires of participants, prepare to burn or bury these symbols. Participants take turns talking briefly about their symbols. Then each participant buries or burns the symbol. After each one finishes, the whole community joins hands and gives the following response:

Let go of your memory and its hold on you.
Your memory will live no longer
   to bring you sorrow and suffering.
Let go in faith that new life awaits you.
Joining hands with you,
   we feel Christ-Sophia, the Spirit of new life.

Words of Comfort

Reader 1 Those who go out weeping,
   bearing the seed for sowing,
   shall come home with shouts of joy,
   carrying their sheaves (Psalm 126:6).

Reader 2 What is sown is perishable;
   what is raised is imperishable.
It is sown in dishonor;
   it is raised in glory.
It is sown in weakness;
   it is raised in power.
It is sown a physical body;
   it is raised a spiritual body (1 Corinthians 15:42–44).

Reader 3 Weeping may linger for the night,
   but joy comes with the morning (Psalm 30:5b).

Reader 4 Blessed are those who mourn,
   for they will be comforted (Matthew 5:4).

Reader 5   Even though I walk through the darkest valley,
        I fear no evil;
    For you are with me;
        your rod and your staff—
        they comfort me (Psalm 23:4).

Reader 6   Comfort, O comfort my people, says your God.
    Speak tenderly to Jerusalem…
    Every valley shall be lifted up,
        and every mountain and hill be made low;
        the uneven ground shall become level,
        and the rough places a plain (Isaiah 40:1–2a, 4).

Reader 7   Blessed is the Spirit of all comfort,
        who comforts us in all our losses,
    So that we may be able to comfort those
        who suffer any loss
        with the comfort with which
        we ourselves are comforted by the Spirit.
    For as we share in the sufferings of Christ-Sophia,
        so also our comfort
        is abundant through Christ-Sophia (based on 2 Corinthians 1:3–5).

Hymn of Comfort   "Share Our Grief, O Christ-Sophia," #29

Prayer of Comfort *(in unison)*

        Spirit of all comfort,
            we have felt your comfort
            through the touch and words of one another.
        As we have held on to some memories and let go of others,
            we have felt your power and peace.
        Christ-Sophia, giver of new life,
            send us forth with the assurance that
            our letting go is a holy act,
        An act of faith that lifts us into fuller life,
            as a seed lets go and is carried aloft by gentle breezes
            to a place where it finds fertile ground
            to become a new flower.

        May we go forth with renewed faith in that day
            when you will wipe away every tear from our eyes,
            and death shall be no more,
        Neither shall there be mourning
            nor crying, nor pain anymore (Revelation 21:4).

BLESSING OF A NEWBORN BABY

Plan this service to be intergenerational. Children and adults form a circle around the baby and parent/s.

Opening Hymn of Celebration "Praise Ruah, Spirit Who Gives Birth," #25; first two stanzas

Meditation on Creation
One person in the group reads the following meditation aloud.

Sisters and brothers, we come together for a most sacred and joyous occasion. We come to celebrate the gift of creation. In the beginning the great Creator birthed the whole universe. The Spirit gave birth to all beings. The Spirit's Hebrew name is *Ruah*. She gave her blessing to all she had birthed, saying, "You are good!" (Genesis 1:1–24)

Ruah gave birth to human beings, making us in her own image; she created male and female in her own image. And she gave us her richest blessing, saying, "Indeed, you are very good!" (Genesis 1:31) From the beginning, we have been blessed. Our Creator blessed us when she birthed us.

The prophet Isaiah reveals that God is like a mother who not only gives birth to children, but who comforts and nurtures them toward their full potential (Isaiah 66:13). God is a nursing mother whose bond with her children is so strong that nothing can sever it (Isaiah 49:15). Our Creator is also like a father who

has compassion for his children (Psalm 103:13; Isaiah 63:15–16). God is a father who lets go of his children and forgives them when they fail (Luke 15:11–32). Our Mother-Father Creator teaches us to walk and heals us when we fall down (Hosea 11:3).

Today we come to praise our Mother-Father Creator as we rejoice in the birth of (name of baby). We gather to celebrate the blessing which our Creator has already placed upon (name of baby). (Name of baby) is a precious (daughter or son) of God, created in the divine image with creative gifts beyond our imagining.

As family both by blood and by faith, we gather to celebrate the blessing of (name of baby) and to covenant to do all in our power to nurture (name of baby) toward all God created (her or him) to be. In doing so, we affirm that (name of baby) is not a gift to us, but a gift living among us. We do not possess (name of baby), but simply rejoice in (her or his) presence among us.

Individual Blessings

Participants take turns giving their blessings to the baby and parent/s. These blessings can take a variety of forms, depending on the faith traditions of the parent/s and the individuals giving the blessings. Some may perform blessings by placing water on the baby's head, similar to baptismal rituals in many traditions. Others may simply place hands of blessing on the baby's head. A small gift may accompany the blessing. Each individual speaks a blessing over the child, choosing one of the following blessings or one of her or his own.

(Name of baby), I bless you in the name of Holy Ruah, our Creator.

(Name of baby), I bless you in the name of our Mother-Father Creator, Redeemer, and Comforter.

(Name of baby), may the One who blessed you with creation continually bless and keep you as you grow toward your fullness in the divine image.

(Name of baby), I celebrate your creation in the divine image and promise to affirm your growth toward your full potential.

(Name of baby), may the Creative Spirit who lives within you nurture and guide you as you develop your creative gifts.

(Name of baby), you have my fullest blessing and my solemn promise to give you affirmation and freedom to become all you were created to be.

(Name of baby), may the Spirit who gave birth to you and who lives within you empower your creative growth as long as you live.

(Name of baby), I affirm the blessing our Mother-Father Creator has already placed upon you and promise to support you as you fulfill your highest potential.

Community Blessing *(read responsively)*

Reader 1   Creation continually happens. New creation always surprises us, bringing us blessing and hope beyond our expectations.

All   We celebrate the new creation in our midst. The miracle of creation lies before us in the form of a precious newborn baby.

Reader 2   This tiny creation mirrors the divine image. We are amazed as we behold the sacred image in (name of baby).

All   As we give you our blessing, (name of baby), we rejoice in the blessing and hope your very being brings us.

Reader 3   (Name of baby), we join together now to celebrate and bless your creation.

All   (Name of baby), we rejoice that you are here! Your birth is a great blessing to us all. We thank the Spirit who created you, and we affirm our faith that this same Creative Spirit lives within you. We offer to surround you with steadfast, unconditional love. We promise to give you the physical, mental, emotional, and spiritual freedom to become the individual you were created to be.

Reader 4   (Name of parent/s), we offer our blessing and support to you as you nurture (name of baby).

All   (Name of parent/s), we rejoice with you in the birth of (name of baby)! We share your excitement! We offer ourselves to be family with you for (name of baby). We promise to surround you with affirmation and love as you become the parent/s you were created to be.

Parent/s   With gratitude (I or we) accept your blessing and support. (Name of baby), your birth brings (me or us) great joy! (I or we) rejoice that you have come to live in (my or our) home. You are a great gift, but not one for (me or us) to possess. You are in the divine image. The Creative Spirit lives in you. (I or we) promise to give you the physical, mental, emotional, and spiritual freedom to become the individual you were created to be.

All   Holy Ruah, Creator of us all, we come to you with awe as we celebrate the miracle of creation. Today we feel a special sense of gratitude for your creation of (name of baby). (She or he) is an amazing creation in your own image. We rejoice in the blessing you have already placed upon (name of baby) when you created (her or him). We know that you live within (her or him), and thus (she or he) has creative potential beyond our imagining. Give us wisdom and grace never to stifle, but to affirm the gifts you have given (her or him). May we join you in helping (her or him) grow into the fullness of all you created (her or him) to be.

CELEBRATION OF DIVERSITY

This service may be intergenerational. Gather in a circle in a large room or outdoors, depending on the weather. In the center of the circle place an altar. On the altar place plants of many varieties and pictures of a variety of animals; find as many unusual plants and animals as possible. Also on the altar place pictures of people of many different races and ages, and pictures of different kinds of families and couples. As participants are arriving, play "We Are the World" or "Jesus Loves the Little Children."

Call to Celebration *(from Psalms 104 and 148)*

Reader 1   How manifold are the works of Sophia, our wise and marvelous Creator!

All   Our Creator loves variety.

Reader 2   The earth is full of wonderful creatures, innumerable living beings both small and large.

All   Our Creator loves variety.

Reader 3   Springs gush forth in valleys rich, nourishing all kinds of wild animals.

All   Our Creator loves variety.

Reader 4   High mountains provide a home for the wild goats, and the rocks give refuge to the coneys.

All   Our Creator loves variety.

Reader 5   The earth is filled with abundant fruit trees and cedars, all kinds of creeping things and flying birds!

All   Our Creator loves variety.

Reader 6   Human beings of varied races and ages fill the earth. No two people have the same fingerprints.

All   Our Creator loves variety.

Reader 7   Couples, families, and communities of many shapes and styles fill the world with love and laughter.

All   Our Creator loves variety.

The Straight-Haired Cocker Spaniel
One person reads the following story to the community.

Once there was a straight-haired cocker spaniel named Flossie, who lived in a small village with a kind family. The family treated Flossie well, giving her anything she wanted to eat and letting her sleep in the house when the weather was cold. Flossie loved this family, especially enjoying the way they stroked her soft black coat and rubbed her smooth stomach. But Flossie soon realized there was more to life than eating and stomach rubs.

So Flossie began to venture out of the yard, running all around town looking for something more. Many times her family went in search of her, fearing that she was lost. Finally, to keep her safe in the backyard, they built a fence. But Flossie dug holes under the fence and escaped to seek her destiny.

When she came back this time, they tied her on a long leash to the clothesline. Flossie was not only a smart dog, but she was also determined to pursue her dreams. The leash was only a minor obstacle to overcome. Before long she had somehow managed to get her head out of the collar that held her to the leash. Off she ran again to find her land.

One lovely spring morning Flossie found a group of cocker spaniels gathered in a park near a river, surrounded by dogwood trees and hot pink azaleas. As she stood on the outside of the group and listened, she knew she had found what she had been searching for. Here was a group who sang and spoke of a joy and freedom beyond any she had imagined. And they celebrated unity and love for all beings. Deep within her soul, Flossie felt her longing become joy, and she began to sing along with them.

Suddenly the singing stopped. All eyes turned to look at Flossie. Embarrassed and shy, Flossie lowered her head and muttered something about wanting to be part of the group. All the dogs continued to stare at Flossie. After a long pause, the leader of the group said, "Well, of course, you understand that we would like you to be a member of our group. But there's one problem. Now we don't want you to take this personally, but your hair is straight. It's not natural for cocker spaniels to have straight hair. You can be in this group only if you change your hair so that it's curly the way it's supposed to be. If you really want to be one of us, we'll help you change your straight hair to curly hair. Do you want to change?"

Flossie's spirit sank as she replied, "Change? I don't understand. I heard you singing and preaching about love and acceptance of all cre-

ated beings. This is the way Sophia, wise Creator of all, made me. Why should I change?"

The leader responded, "We believe all cocker spaniels are created to be curly-haired. That's what our sacred laws teach. It's unnatural for a cocker spaniel to have straight hair. But come on and join our group, and we'll help make your hair curly."

By this time Flossie was so confused that she didn't know the right thing to do. One part of her was crying out to stay in this holy place and to belong in this group. But another part of her spirit was protesting their need to change her hair. If all cocker spaniels are created to be curly-haired, as the leader had said, why was she straight-haired? What was wrong with her? Should she try to change her hair, and would she be able to change it?

Flossie's need for belonging won out, and she said, "All right. I really want to join your group. I'll try as hard as I can to change my hair." The group took her in, and immediately started preaching to her about ways to make her straight hair curly. They were all earnest and determined to help her change. They advised her as to books she could read on making straight hair curly, products she could use, and those who could help her.

For many years Flossie worked diligently to make her straight hair curly. She spent a great deal of time and money trying to change her hair. Some things she tried seemed to help for a little while. Before the meeting of the holy community every week, she spent hours working on her hair to make it curly. When she went to the meeting, the other cocker spaniels praised her, saying, "How pretty you look today, Flossie. Curly hair does become you!" Flossie would smile and say, "Thank you." But deep down she felt sad and lonely. She didn't feel like herself with curly hair.

And no matter how hard Flossie tried to keep her hair curly, it didn't last long. Sometimes even before the end of the holy meetings, her curls would begin to sag. And she would feel embarrassed and ashamed.

One day Flossie awoke and looked in the mirror and said to herself, "I'm a straight-haired, not a curly-haired, cocker spaniel. That's the way the wise Sophia created me, and I like the way I am. I'm beautiful just the way I am with my straight black hair. I'm not going to try to curl it anymore."

Flossie went to the next meeting of the holy community with hair clean and shiny and straight. Some of the cocker spaniels whispered and pointed at her. But she marched proudly up to the front of the group and sat down. After the meeting, the leaders of the community had another meeting to discuss what to do about Flossie. They decided that since she had been a faithful member of the community, giving valuable service for many years, she could stay. But they would tell her they expected her to continue to try to change her hair.

The leaders met with Flossie and told her this decision. She replied, "The community is important to me. Your message of freedom and joy inspires and warms my soul. But you're not living your message. You're not giving me freedom to be who I'm created to be. I'll stay in the community. I feel called to be a leader so that I can preach this message and create rituals to act out this message."

The head leader quickly responded, "Oh, no! That will not do at all! We could never allow you to preach or to handle the sacred bones." The other leaders chimed in, "No, no! Never can you be a leader! Only curly-haired cocker spaniels can be leaders. Only curly-haired cocker spaniels can touch the sacred bones." Flossie hung her head. Large tears welled up in her eyes, and she walked away in silence.

After months of trying to run away from her community and her pain, Flossie knew what she had to do. She knew she couldn't go back to being a kept dog, no matter how good the food and stomach rubs had been. She had searched too long and hard for something more. Her spirit had been awakened, and she could not go back. But how could she stay in a community that didn't believe she was good enough to handle sacred things?

Her holy anger gave her the answer.

When the day for the next meeting of the community came, Flossie walked right up to the front with head held high. Filled with the spirit of Sophia, Flossie began to speak: "How dare you say that only curly-haired cocker spaniels can handle sacred things? Our all-wise Creator made us all—straight-haired and curly-haired, cocker spaniels and beagles, even cats and roaches. Curly-haired cocker spaniels do not have a monopoly on the spiritual. You may cut me off from this community, but you cannot cut me off from the sacred. Whether in this community or somewhere else, I will create sacred rituals. I will be a holy leader. For I am holy."

Flossie became a holy leader. Animals of all kinds and hair-types and shapes came from far and wide to learn wisdom from Flossie.

Hymn of Contemplation   "O Flower Blooming in Deepest Pain," #21

Invite participants to talk about feelings stirred by the story, "The Straight-Haired Cocker Spaniel," and/or the hymn, "O Flower Blooming in Deepest Pain."

Prayer of Confession *(in unison)*

Wise and wonderful Creator of infinite variety,
     forgive our petty striving to squeeze you
     and your creation into our conventions.
Sophia, flower of richest and rarest beauty,
     forgive our ignorance and prejudice
     that has kept us from seeing your sacredness.
Though you created us with wondrous diversity,
     we have tried to restrict one another
     into limited ways of being and doing,
     and we are all the losers.

Forgive us and heal us of our racism,
   heterosexism, sexism, classism,
   and all other evils that keep us
   from appreciating your abundant, manifold creation. Amen.

Covenant to Celebrate Diversity

Reader 1   Sophia, our wise and marvelous Creator, fills the earth with amazing diversity.

All   We covenant with our Creator and with one another to celebrate and nurture diversity.

Reader 2   Innumerable living beings fill the earth, beyond our ability to fathom or classify.

All   We covenant with our Creator and with one another to celebrate and nurture diversity.

Reader 3   Mountains and valleys, forests and oceans, sing forth the abundance of creation.

All   We covenant with our Creator and with one another to celebrate and nurture diversity.

Reader 4   Ostriches and otters, amphipods and anteaters, show forth the playful prodigality of our Creator.

All   We covenant with our Creator and with one another to celebrate and nurture diversity.

Reader 5   Human beings of rich colors and shapes show forth the lavishness of our Creator.

All   We covenant with our Creator and with one another to celebrate and nurture diversity.

Reader 6   Our Creator loves variety, and so created people to express sexuality in different ways.

All   We covenant with our Creator and with one another to celebrate and nurture diversity.

Reader 7   Families and communities of diverse forms and cultures fill the world with joy and grace.

All   We covenant with our Creator and with one another to celebrate and nurture diversity.

Hymn of Celebration   "Celebrate a New Day Dawning," #1

CELEBRATION OF ALL SAINTS' DAY

Before the service, ask each participant to bring a picture of someone, living or deceased, whom she/he considers to be a saint. Gather in a circle around an altar on which are placed one large candle in a holder in the center and ten smaller candles in holders around it. Surround the candles in fresh foliage from evergreen trees. As the service begins, play soft music for meditation, while giving everyone a candle.

Invoking the Spirit of All Saints

One person lights the large candle in the center of the altar, while the whole community reads the following prayer in unison.

> Spirit, who inspires all saints,
>   come to our gathering here this day.
> For all saints, past and present,
>   who have been faithful to the vision
>   you have blazed within them,
>   we are thankful.
> Light the fire of your vision within us,
>   so that we too will be your faithful saints,
>   now and always. Amen.

Celebration of Sister Saints Past

Individuals read the following poems. Before each reads a poem, she or he takes one of the small candles on the altar, lights it from the large candle in the center, and places it back in its holder on the altar.

Hildegard of Bingen (1098-1179)

> Hildegard of Bingen, preacher to priests,
>   you followed your heavenly vision
>   beyond the bounds of your time and gender.
> You challenged religious and civil authorities,
>   prophesying to popes, bishops, emperors, and kings
>   concerning the truth and justice revealed
>   in your visions.
>
> Sister Hildegard, your gifted mind and unquenchable energy
>   burst forth like fireworks
>   in poetry, drama, and songs,
>   theological, historical, political, and medical volumes.
> Sibyl of the Rhine, your stellar work,

ignored by generations who demeaned the "feminine mind,"
    shines down to us with true brilliance.

Mother of medicine, you discovered a treatment for diabetes
    and discussed the circulation of blood,
        yet the fathers of medicine took credit.
Progressive for your day and for our own,
    you combined prayer and herbal medicine,
        bringing East and West together
        for the healing of the whole body-mind-spirit.

Infused with divine Sophia,
    before her inspiration was questioned,
    your whole being glowed with the divine light of Wisdom,
    and you wrote your visions of splendor and glory.
Saint Hildegard, you opened yourself for miracles
    to flow forth from you
    in a fountain of mystical beauty.

Julian of Norwich (1343-1423)

Sister Julian, faithful daughter of the church,
    mother of new revelations,
    you spoke the truth of your visions.
As a window open to fresh morning light,
    you opened yourself to new "shewings,"
    letting them flood your soul with insight
    into reality.

In your vision you saw not only divine Fatherhood,
    but divine Motherhood.
"All-Wisdom is our kindly Mother,"[13] you proclaimed,
    a radical proclamation for the fourteenth century and even for the twentieth.
For centuries you were dismissed and scorned
    as unstable, uneducated, ignorant of the weightier matters of the church.
Your "shewings" were ignored and buried.

But saints will not stay buried.
You rose, Saint Julian, from your obscure grave
    to lead us to fuller light.
You stand in a long line of prophetic saints who witness larger visions:
    the Holy One in a burning bush;
    the Divine Creator in human flesh;
    the Sacred Spirit in feminine form.

Saint Julian, you opened yourself
    to startling, sacred revelations;
    you claimed and proclaimed your revolutionary truth.

You opened the way for all who see
    to stand on holy ground,
    incarnate holy love,
    and proclaim liberating truth.

Sojourner Truth (c. 1797-1883)

Isabelle, born a slave in New York,
    freed at last to claim your name from God,
    you became Sojourner Truth.
Following your divine call,
    you gave up safety to sojourn from place to place,
    preaching truth's message
    of freedom for all people.

Sister Sojourner, not resting in your own freedom,
    you risked your life to preach release from slavery,
    as you sang your song,
"I am pleading that my people,
    may have their rights restored;
    for they have long been toiling,
    and yet have no reward."[14]

Truth-Deliverer, brave Sojourner,
    your vision of justice included women,
    enslaved in culture and religion that included only men.
Like a mighty ocean tide,
    you washed over shores of tradition with your bold words:
"And how came Jesus into the world? Through God who created him
    and a woman who bore him. Man, where is your part?"[15]

Saint Sojourner, though not labeled such,
    you remained true to your vision
    of justice and freedom for all.
Liberator of slaves by race and gender,
    you inspire us with faith and courage
    to claim our true names and
    to follow sacred truth.

Susan B. Anthony (1820-1906)

Susan B. Anthony, gentle Quaker woman,
    mother of a revolution,
    you refused to be refused the vote,
    and stirred women across the country to refuse.
You led women from passive to active resistance,
    wise Susan, embodiment of Sophia,
    before you knew her name.

Woman of Wisdom, Sister Susan,
　　you followed the inner light
　　guiding you to liberty and justice.
You spoke your truth that became our truth:
"It was we, the people, not we...the male citizens...who formed this
Union.... to give the blessings of liberty...not to the half of ourselves and the
half of our posterity, but to the whole people—women as well as men."[16]

Mother of freedom, Susan B. Anthony,
　　we have valued you too lightly.
Your image, stamped on one-dollar coins, almost out of circulation
　　is small compensation for fifty years of tireless work
　　to change an unjust system.
You deserve at least a one-day national celebration,
　　like Martin Luther King, Jr.

Courageous and saintly Susan,
　　as the pilgrims who came to find religious liberty in a new world,
　　you set out with divine determination blazing in your eyes
　　to claim women's rights to our land.
Too soon have we forgotten your hard-won victories,
　　too easily let your voice and ours fade away
　　like echoes in a dark cave.

Harriet Tubman (c. 1820-1913)

Harriet Tubman, called the Moses of your people,
　　you followed your vision of liberation,
　　leading your people out of bondage
　　into the Promised Land of freedom.
With rare courage you led over three hundred slaves
　　out of America's Egypt,
　　risking your life to let your people go.

Struck unconscious by a cruel pharoah in Maryland,
　　you first determined to make your own exodus.
Free at last, you exclaimed,
　　"I looked at my hands to see if I was the same person now I was free.
　　There was such a glory over everything.
　　The sun came like gold through the trees and over the fields,
　　and I felt like I was in heaven."[17]

Not content to bask in the glory of your own freedom,
　　you answered the divine call to help others
　　run away from slavery by the Underground Railroad.
On another sacred mission of freedom,
　　you joined Susan B. Anthony and other suffragists,
　　encouraging sisters to stick together to gain the right to vote,

assuring them that God was on their side.
Sister Harriet, like brother Moses and
   sister Miriam before you,
   you trusted supernatural power to break bonds
   of oppression and slavery.
If miracles make saints,
   then you are Saint Harriet.
Your whole life overflowed with miracles.

Hymn of Celebration   "Our Sister Saints"
This hymn is sung to the hymn setting SINE NOMINE, *also known as "For All the Saints."*

Our sister saints who from their labor rest
With faith and courage led the justice-quest.
Their work, O Christ-Sophia, you have blessed.
Alleluia, Alleluia.

You were companion in their joy and pain;
Your presence proof their work was not in vain.
O Mother Christ, to hope give birth again.
Alleluia, Alleluia.

O may we join these sisters from before,
Speak as one voice, define one holy chore;
Take up the call for justice evermore.
Alleluia, Alleluia.

And when we falter from our labor long,
Share with us still your shining grace-full song,
That hearts are brave again and voices strong.
Alleluia, Alleluia.

Words © 1996 Sally Browder and Jann Aldredge-Clanton

Celebration of Brother Saints Past

Individuals read the following poems. Before each reads a poem, he or she takes one of the small candles on the altar, lights it from the large candle in the center, and places it back in its holder on the altar.

Francis of Assisi (c. 1181-1226)

Francis of Assisi, born to wealth,
   you gave up all privilege for a life of poverty, simplicity, and humility.
Denounced as a madman by your father,
   you stripped yourself of earthly possessions
     to possess a greater glory and honor.
Led by your love of Lady Poverty,

you gave richly to help the poor and hurting.
Brother Francis, playful lover of life,
   you believed all creation connected by divine love and beauty.
Feeling your deep kinship with all living beings,
   you addressed swallows as brothers and sisters,
   refused to step on an earthworm in your path,
   took a struggling carp from a fisherman's hand
   and returned it to its watery home.

Seeing the equality of male and female in the created order,
   you welcomed Saint Clare as sister in the faith and praised
   Sister Moon along with Brother Sun,
   Sister Water and Brother Fire,
   Sister Earth and Brother Wind.
Brother Francis, you valued
   the sacredness of sisters and brothers alike.

Saint Francis, though you humbly
   called yourself "little black hen,"
   you are a saint indeed.
With a gentle peacemaking spirit,
   you held fast your values and your vision
   of the divine path to love
   for all creation.

Meister Eckhart (1260-1327)

Meister Eckhart, founder of the Friends of God,
   you proved a friend to all.
With eyes open
   to those in need around you,
   you worked actively with the oppressed,
   believing in Martha's part,
   as well as Mary's.

Mystic Meister Eckhart, you saw
   divinity in all creation,
   even in flies.
Believing in a radical equality of being,
   you taught love and reverence for all, proclaiming,
   "All things possess existence immediately
   and equally from God alone."[18]

Brother Eckhart, embracing the divine image in all,
   you celebrated and nurtured mystical gifts in sisters
   as well as in brothers.
Affirming our connection with divine Sophia,
   you understood human creativity
   as reflecting and delighting
   the constantly creating Creator.

Condemned by the church
   though you should have been canonized,
   you are Saint Eckhart.
Spiritual Seer, prophesying beyond tradition,
   you spoke a new word
   of eternal reality
   at the foundation of the universe.

John of the Cross (1542-1591)

John of the Cross, born to a silk weaver,
   you became a weaver of rich tapestries,
   mingling threads of darkness and light.
You sang of going forth on a "joyous night,"
   a "night more loving than the dawn,"
   with no light but the fire burning in your heart,
   guiding you "more directly than the midday sun."[19]

Brother John, closely collaborating with Sister Teresa,
   you brought spiritual reform
   through your gifts of mysticism,
   pragmatism, and strong will.
Refreshed and strengthened at the fount of eternal Sophia,
   you and Teresa in mutual ministry
   served as spiritual director to each other.

In spite of violent opposition,
   imprisonment, and persecution for your efforts
   to revitalize your religious community,
   you refused to renounce
   your divine mission.
Miraculously escaping from prison,
   you stayed faithful to your vision.

John of the Cross, humble mystic and saint,
   you taught possession of everything by owning nothing.
Saint John, through the beautiful simplicity
   of your poetry and your life,
   you showed us the way
   through the "dark night of the soul"
   into light and love.

John Stuart Mill (1806-1873)

John Stuart Mill, champion of liberty,
   honestly grappling with political and religious issues,
   you taught a morality of justice.
Believing in the free development and exercise

of gifts and virtues as vital to human well-being,
   you denounced the desire for power
   that led to the subjection of any individuals.

Brother Mill, opposer of oppression,
   with your strong words you exposed the evil
   of the most prevalent form, the subjection of women:
   "Subordination of one sex to the other...is wrong in itself, and
   now one of the chief hindrances to human improvement...it ought
   to be replaced by a principle of perfect equality, admitting
   no power or privilege on the one side, nor disability on the other."[20]

Challenging the sacred status of patriarchy,
   associating it with idol worship, paganism, and false religion,
   you advocated the emancipation of women and men
   from patriarchal institutions that corrupt all.
Justice-maker, as a member of Parliament in Victorian England,
   you pushed for women's suffrage,
   in spite of harsh criticism and hostility.

John Stuart Mill, lover of liberty,
   compassionate and eloquent
   advocate of human rights,
   your saintly devotion
   to the divine vision of justice
   shines a beacon of hope
   on our storm-weary land.

Martin Luther King, Jr. (1929-1968)

Martin Luther King, Jr., visionary in action,
   you preached nonviolent opposition to racism.
Challenging racial discrimination and
   violent means of opposing racism,
   you led peaceful demonstations and freedom walks.
In spite of bombings and stabbings and stonings,
   you never carried even a pocketknife to defend yourself.

Prophet Martin, you proclaimed
   your dream of a nation where children
   "will not be judged by the color of their skin
   but by the content of their character."[21]
Including social justice for the poor in your vision,
   you preached and worked
   for better housing and jobs.

Brother Martin, eloquent dreamer,
   you worked closely with Sister Dorothy Cotton,

who followed your teaching to its ethical conclusion
of gender as well as racial liberation,
believing you would grow to see women also as an oppressed class.
In the face of severe criticism, you kept your commitment
to nonviolence by opposing the Vietnam War.

Faithfulness to your divine dream
led you through suffering and death.
Your spirit lives on, Saint Martin;
your words come down to us like manna
as we move toward that land
where we will all be
free at last.

Hymn of Celebration   "Our Brother Saints"
This hymn is sung to the hymn setting SINE NOMINE, *also known as "For All the Saints."*

Our brother saints who from their labor rest
Through actions proved the justice they professed.
Their work, O Christ-Sophia, you have blessed.
Alleluia, Alleluia.

You held and nurtured them throughout the night;
O Christ-Sophia, you gave them new sight.
Led by your vision, they preached truth and right.
Alleluia, Alleluia.

These brothers saw the world through mystic eyes;
they loved all beings, heard the poorest cries.
Like them, O Christ-Sophia, make us wise.
Alleluia, Alleluia.

O may we join these brothers from the past,
With gentle strength, hold our convictions fast,
That freedom's song we all may sing at last,
Alleluia, Alleluia.

Words © 1996 Jann Aldredge-Clanton

Celebration of our Personal Saints

One by one, each participant takes the candle she or he received at the beginning of the service and lights this candle from the large candle in the center of the altar. Holding the candle in one hand and the picture of the person he or she considers to be a saint in the other, each talks briefly about the saint, telling why she/he chose that person.

Parting Blessing of All Saints

Group 1   Many sister saints have gone before us to light the way to justice and freedom. In spite of danger and suffering and limitations, they stayed faithful to their divine vision.

All   For all the sister saints who have gone before us, we are grateful. We bless them as they have blessed us.

Group 2   Many brother saints have gone before us to light the way to justice and freedom. In spite of danger and suffering and limitations, they stayed faithful to their divine vision.

All   For all the brother saints who have gone before us, we are grateful. We bless them as they have blessed us.

Group 1   Sister and brother saints still present in our lives show us the way of truth and justice and love and wholeness and harmony, as they nurture our gifts and our dreams.

Group 2   Sister and brother saints still present risk opposition and suffering and danger to live out their vision of a new creation of freedom and power for all.

All   For all the sister and brother saints still present in our lives, we are grateful. We bless them as they bless us.

Group 1   All of us in this community are saints. In spite of danger and suffering and limitations, we challenge unjust systems and institutions with our prophetic visions.

Group 2   All of us gathered in this community are saints, for we envision a better way, a way of justice and wholeness and creative beauty flowing freely from all.

All   For this community we are grateful, for we are all saints. We bless one another.

Participants exchange hugs and words of blessing.

All   For all saints past and present, for those in this world and those in the world beyond, for all saints near and far, we thank you, Christ-Sophia, fountain of Wisdom, from whom all saints flow. Send us forth filled with your Spirit, so that we may speak freely and live faithfully the truth of our visions, for we are all saints. Amen.

THANKSGIVING FOR GIFTS RECEIVED & GIFTS GIVEN

This service may be intergenerational. Before the service, ask each adult participant to bring two symbols: one symbol of some gift they received in the past year that contributed to their creative empowerment, and one symbol of some gift they plan to give for the empowerment of some oppressed person or persons. Ask each child to bring a gift they received that they are grateful for and a gift they plan to give to someone else.

Sit in a circle in a large room or outdoors, if the weather is temperate. In the center of the circle, create an altar with fresh flowers, a cornucopia filled with fresh fruits and vegetables, bright-colored leaves fresh-fallen from trees, a pot of hot apple cider, and cups for each participant. As participants arrive, play celebratory music.

Call to Thanksgiving *(based on Genesis 1)*

Leader   In the beginning Ruah moved over the face of the waters and said, "Let there be light," and there was light. And Ruah said, "It is good."

All   The light is good. Thanks be to Ruah!

Leader   And Ruah created the earth, dividing the dry land from the seas. And Ruah said, "It is good."

All   The earth is good. Thanks be to Ruah!

Leader   Then Ruah gave birth to vegetation, all kinds of plants and trees bearing fruit. And Ruah said, "It is good."

All   The vegetation is good. Thanks be to Ruah!

Leader   And Ruah created the sun and the moon and the stars. And Ruah said, "They are good."

All   The sun and the moon and the stars are good. Thanks be to Ruah!

Leader   Then Ruah gave birth to all the fish, both large and small, that swim in the oceans and to all the winged birds that fly above the earth. And Ruah said, "They are good."

All   The fish and the birds are good. Thanks be to Ruah!

Leader   And Ruah gave birth to the cattle and to all the animals that live on the ground. Then Ruah gave birth to human beings; in her own image she created them female and male. And Ruah asked them to take good care of all the other living beings she had created. For Ruah said, "They are all good."

All   Human beings, female and male, and all other living beings are good. Thanks be to Ruah!

Leader   Then Ruah was tired after so much creating, and she sat down to rest. Relaxing, she took a deep breath, and then she breathed out into us her Spirit of creativity as she invited us to continue her creation. And Ruah said, "All that I create is good. You are in my image, and all that you create with me is good. Accept my gift of creativity."

All   Ruah, Spirit of all creation, all that you create is good. We are in your image, and all that we create with you is good. We accept your gift of creativity. Thanks be to you, O Ruah!

Hymn of Praise   "Praise Ruah, Spirit Who Gives Birth," #25
Sing with hand movements.

Psalms of Thanksgiving

Reader 1   Sing joyful songs to Ruah, who created the earth and every living being. Worship Ruah with glad singing and dancing. Know that Ruah is holy; her presence surrounds us and fills us with goodness and grace; her steadfast love endures forever (based on Psalm 100).

Reader 2   It is good to give thanks to you, Giver of all good gifts, to sing praises to your name, to declare your steadfast love in the morning and your faithfulness by night. The beauty of your creation makes our hearts glad; we sing for joy when we gaze upon earth's splendor. We will dance and sing our thanks to you; we will make music to show our gratitude. How great are your works, O creative Spirit; the works of your hands make our hearts glad (based on Psalm 92:1–5).

Reader 3   Bless Ruah, Spirit of all creation. O Ruah, we give thanks to you. Clothed with purple garments of light, you move over land and water, bringing forth multiform life and beauty. Riding on the wings of the wind, you make chariot clouds in the sky. You make the moon to mark the seasons, and the sun to rise at daybreak. You make springs gush forth in the valleys, flowing through the hills, giving drink to every wild animal. Great Creator, you give grass for the cattle and plants for people to eat. You make mountains for the wild goats and trees for the birds to build their nests. Wisdom-worker, you make the lions roar and the whales sport in the wide seas. You make the darkness of night for the animals of the forest to come creeping out. The earth is filled with your creations, innumerable living beings, both small and large. May your glory endure forever; may you rejoice in all your works. We will sing to you as long as we live. All wise and creative Spirit, we will sing praise to you forever (based on Psalm 104).

Reader 4 Sing to the Creator a new song; make melody and dance for joy. Sing songs of thanksgiving to the One with many names; make new songs to praise the vastness of the Creator: sing a new song to Ruah, Spirit of creation; sing a new song to *El Shaddai*, the breasted one; sing a new song to the comforting Friend; sing a new song to the Rock of Salvation, sing a new song to the soaring Mother Eagle; sing a new song to the nurturing Mother Hen; sing a new song to the Fountain of all blessings; sing a new song to Mother-Father Creator; sing a new song to Sister-Brother Sustainer; sing a new song to Christ-Sophia, Giver of new life. Let all that hath breath, sing a new song (based on Psalm 149:1–3).

Song of Thanksgiving   "Christ-Sophia Now We Bless," #3, stanzas 1 through 3

Celebrating the Harvest

One of the members of the community pours hot apple cider for everyone. All lift their cups together for a toast, saying the following words together:

> We celebrate the harvest,
>   giving thanks for the fruit of the earth.
> We remember the hungry and oppressed
>   throughout the earth,
>   making a covenant to share our gifts.
> To celebrating and sharing our harvest,
>   we drink.

Damaris and the Nightingales: A Thanksgiving Story

One of the children reads the following story to the community.

In a deep green forest south of Monterrey there lived a flock of nightingales. All nightingales are noted for their melodious songs, but this flock especially prided themselves on the beauty of their singing. Each year at the great feast of Thanksgiving, they would gather to show their gratitude to Ruah, Wind and Spirit, Creator of nightingales and all living beings.

The climax of the feast was the offering of gifts to express appreciation to Ruah. All year long each nightingale worked to perfect a song to bring as a gift to Ruah. Some nightingales sang solos, and some sang together in choirs. All worked hard to bring their best gifts to Ruah.

But none worked any harder than a nightingale named Damaris. Damaris felt embarrassed and ashamed that her voice was lower than the other nightingales' voices. She listened to their melodies, ringing out in notes high and clear, and she tried to match them. But when she came to the highest notes, her voice always cracked.

Every year Damaris dreaded the feast of Thanksgiving. No matter how hard she worked on her song, it never seemed to measure up to the songs of the other nightingales. Through much practice, she learned to sing high notes, but when she came to the highest notes at the climax of her song, her voice would crack. And Damaris would feel embarrassed and frustrated.

Once she tried to sing in one of the choirs. She spent many hours alone, practicing the high melodies. But when she came together with the choir, try as she might, she could not match their high notes. She would be a little off-pitch, and her voice would crack on the highest notes. She felt so embarrassed that she dropped out of the choir.

The time for the annual feast of Thanksgiving was approaching. As usual, Damaris began working on her song long before any of the other nightingales. Several weeks before the feast, she became so anxious that she could hardly eat or sleep.

Her good friend Pytheus tried to encourage her, saying, "Your voice is just as beautiful as any other nightingale's. So what if it's a little lower. Why don't you sing your song in a lower pitch?"

Damaris replied, "Oh no! I could never do that! The other nightingales would not like such a song, and Ruah would not be pleased if I didn't bring her a perfect nightingale song." Damaris continued to work night and day on her song.

The day for the great feast of Thanksgiving arrived. All the nightingales, their reddish-brown feathers preened to perfection, gathered in the center of the forest. Before them were tables sumptuously spread with grains and fruits of every kind. Before the meal, the nightingales took turns offering their best gifts to Ruah, Wind and Spirit, Creator of all nightingales and all living beings. First the choirs of nightingales sang their gifts to Ruah. Their voices joined together to ring out crystal clear notes, more beautiful than Damaris had ever heard. All the nightingales swayed and nodded to their lovely melodies. Then came the solo voices. One after another, they sang forth their high strains with grace and ease.

Then came Damaris' turn. With trembling wings and throat, she began her song. At first her notes were strong and clear. Then as she moved into the high crescendo, her voice cracked. She quickly finished her song, and then flew slowly away, with head hung low.

Her friend Pytheus flew after her, trying to comfort her, "Your song was good," he said to her. "So what if it wasn't perfect. The other songs weren't perfect." But Damaris continued to hang her head, while tears fell from her eyes.

All of a sudden through the wind came a voice, saying, "I am Ruah, Creator of all nightingales and all living beings. Damaris, your song was good. I accept your good gift. I created you and your voice, and all that I create is good. You are in my image, and all that you create is good. I create the good, not the perfect. You're the one who has tried to create the perfect. There is no perfect, only different goods. I've created different beings with different goods so that you will all see your need of one another. Your low voice is the good gift I have given you. The high-voiced nightingales need your voice, just as you need theirs. Sing in your own voice, for it is good." Her friend Pytheus smiled and said, "Amen."

From that day on Damaris sang in a choir of nightingales, her low notes blending with the high notes to make splendid harmony. And this choir of nightingales became known throughout the land for their euphonious music.

Thanksgiving for Gifts Received

Children takes turns expressing thanksgiving for some gift they received in the past year, showing the gift to the community. Adults take turns expressing thanksgiving for some gift they received in the past year that empowered their creativity. As they speak, they show the community the symbol of this gift. After the last person speaks, the whole community speaks the following response in unison:

> Sometimes we find it difficult to receive.
> We often have trouble believing the gifts are for us.
> Today we come believing and receiving.
> We receive these gifts with gratitude for the ways they
>   spark our creativity, bringing us new life.
> We receive these gifts with thanksgiving,
>   knowing that by receiving,
>   we are also giving a blessing to the giver.

Thanksgiving for Gifts Given

Children take turns expressing thanksgiving for some gift they plan to give, placing the gift on the altar. Adults take turns expressing thanksgiving for some gift that they plan to give for the creative empowerment of some oppressed person or persons. After each one speaks, she/he places the symbol of this gift on the altar. After the last person speaks, the whole community speaks the following response in unison:

> Sometimes we forget to notice all the gifts we have to give.
> We compare ourselves to others who seem to have more,
>   and wonder if our gifts are good enough.
> Today we come with gratitude for the gifts we are giving,
>   for the ways they will bring new life and power to others.
> We give these good gifts with thanksgiving,
>   knowing that by giving
>   we are also receiving a blessing from the receiver.

Prayer of Thanksgiving

Group 1 Fountain of bountiful blessings, we come with deep gratitude for opportunities to give and to receive, for eyes to see the beauty of sunsets and the sparkle in the eyes of children, for ears to hear music and laughter, for the smell of fresh-baked bread, for the kiss of fall breezes upon our skin, for the sweet taste of pumpkin pie and other Thanksgiving treats.

Group 2 We also come to remember those children whose eyes cry out their need and whose ears too often hear the growling in their own stomachs and the fighting of those around them who are struggling in poverty. Compassionate Mother-Father of us all, help us to feel the suffering of our sisters and brothers. Challenge us to join you in breaking down barriers of prejudice, injustice, ignorance, and poverty so that all living beings may have the freedom to become all you created us to be.

All Ruah, Spirit of all creation, we come with thanksgiving for your freely flowing gifts that nourish and sustain and bring beauty to our lives. For the continual renewal of our lives through your gifts of creativity and joy, we are indeed grateful. For gifts to give we are also grateful, knowing that as we give we also receive. Dancing in your circle of giving and receiving, we become united with you and with all creation.

Christ-Sophia, may we freely give from all that we have received, following your example of wise and creative compassion, justice-making, and peacemaking. May we experience your presence in fresh ways as we come together in creative partnership. May our connections with you and with one another empower us to be your agents of change in our community and in our world, through your gracious spirit. Amen.

Song of Thanksgiving and Challenge   "Christ-Sophia Now We Bless," #3, stanza 4

BIRTHING CHRIST-SOPHIA

Plan this service to be intergenerational. Gather in a circle around an altar. On the altar place candles in holders, holly, and poinsettia. Also place on the altar symbols of birthing, such as Lamaze manuals, wet towels, and unfinished manuscripts, paintings, and other projects. As participants are gathering, play soft music. Just before beginning the service, light the candles.

Invoking the Divine Midwife

Voice 1   Giving birth is hard work.

All   O Divine Midwife, we need your help.

Voice 2   Giving birth is frightening.

All   O Divine Midwife, we need your comfort.

Voice 3   Giving birth is painful.

All   O Divine Midwife, we need your relief.

Voice 4   We are giving birth to new words and new rituals.

All   O Divine Midwife, we need your creativity.

Voice 5   We are giving birth to Christ-Sophia, a new word and a new wisdom for mutual relationship.

All   O Divine Midwife, we need your partnership in this birthing.

Voice 6   Giving birth brings excitement and great joy.

All   O Divine Midwife, we patiently labor with you, through the long night of pain and fear, holding onto your comforting hand, pushing and breathing with all our might, until the Womb of all Creation opens and Christ-Sophia comes forth, wrapped in refreshing waters of liberation and wholeness and beauty. Then all creation will sing of glory in the highest heavens and peace on earth.

Hymn of Expectation   "O Come, Christ-Sophia," #19

A Story of Comings

One of the children reads the following story to the community.

A long time ago, in a time outside of time, Sophia and Logos danced together in perfect balance and beauty, diversity and unity. Sophia and Logos were separate but connected. Sophia, whose name means "wisdom," and Logos, whose name means "word," knew that they needed each other. Sophia knew that she found expression in Logos, and Logos knew that he found meaning in Sophia. Together they gave birth to the whole universe.

Logos and Sophia danced the stars into light. Skipping in and out of starlight and moonglow, they waved their hands and separated the waters from the land. As Logos and Sophia continued to dance together in creative unity, flowers began to bloom at their feet and plants of all kinds sprang from the earth. Then hand in hand they ran to the water and dived in.

As they swam and played together, the sea began to teem with fish, both large and small. Full of life and energy, Sophia and Logos jumped out of the water and swung each other around and around, laughing and sprinkling the ground with water from their wet bodies. The moist earth gave birth to more life, wild animals and winged birds of every kind.

Then Logos and Sophia said to each other, "Let's make humankind in our image." So they gave birth to female and male human beings in their own image of perfect balance and beauty, diversity and unity. Sophia and Logos created male and female human beings in their image to live together in mutual relationship. Surveying all the wonders they had created, they danced the whole day long in pure delight.

For many years the human beings lived together in harmony with one another and with all creation. Female and male human beings lived and loved in mutual relationship, nurturing and respecting all other created beings. They worshiped Sophia and Logos, who had created them and all living beings.

They sang hymns to Logos and Sophia, who continually sustained and blessed them with all good things. They believed that Sophia and Logos lived within them, giving them power for all goodness and creativity.

Gradually things began to change. No one knows just why or how.

Everything began to shift out of balance. Harmony and mutuality were no more. Male human beings began to dominate female human beings. Male and female human beings began to abuse and destroy other animals. Sophia's face and name became hidden, as human beings chose to worship only Logos. They abused the image of Logos, using it to sanction wars and violence of all kinds. They supported the dominance of male human beings through their worship of the male Logos alone. They distorted the name of Logos, calling him King and Master to increase the power of their own rulers.

Logos and Sophia, in the land and time beyond, sat down together and wept. How could this have ever happened to their good creation? What could they do now to restore creation to wholeness and peace? Holding hands in silence, they thought until they came up with a plan. Sophia and Logos said to each other, "Let us go into the land and time of all beings we created. We can show them how to live again in loving, mutual relationship."

They talked about going together. Then they looked at each other in sadness as they realized that only Logos would have a chance of restoring this broken land. In this land, ruled by male human beings, the voice of Sophia would be silenced. Violent human beings might even kill Sophia. So they decided that Logos would become a male human being so that he could teach the evil of male dominance and the value of the feminine, thus restoring wholeness to creation.

So Logos became flesh in the land and time of all created beings. He was born in a small town in Judea to a poor couple. He chose such a humble way of coming into this land to subvert the dominant-submissive order that expected a divinely anointed deliverer in the form of a king.

Herod knew Logos was a threat to the rule of kings, and he tried to destroy the baby Logos. But the child lived. A bright star guided followers of Sophia to come and see him. Logos grew in the ways of Sophia, for he was still united with Sophia in the land beyond. Logos went about the land making peace, healing many beings, and teaching the ways of Sophia.

Some created beings understood the teaching of Logos and followed him. But many misunderstood him. They wanted him to be a king and to rule over all the kingdoms of the world. He refused. Logos tried to show a better way in which no one rules over others, but all live in loving partnership. They mocked him, saying, "You're living in a dream world. Who do you think you are? Everyone, come see the dreamer!" Their voices rose louder and louder, mocking and jeering until they thought they had completely silenced Logos. But the true Logos could not be buried beneath their shouts and jeers.

Logos rose again with greater energy to bring justice and peace to the land of all created beings. His followers grew in number and power. At first they followed his ways of justice and mutual relationship. But then they began to reestablish the dominant-submissive order, designating some to rule over others because they believed them to be holier. And they began teaching that because Logos was male, male human beings were superior and should have power over all others.

Violence of all kinds continued to destroy living beings in the land. Although Logos had tried to revive the worship of Sophia, his followers continued to worship only a distorted masculine deity to support the rule of males. Each year they held a month-long feast in celebration of the advent of Logos, but their eyes remained closed to the meaning of his first humble coming into their land, and their minds remained closed to the continual comings of Logos.

Logos and Sophia, in the land and time beyond, sat down together again and wept. What had gone wrong with their plan? Was there still hope for restoring creation to peace and wholeness? Finally, they thought of another plan. This time they would make their coming into the land of created beings together. Sophia was willing to risk the silencing of her voice and even her death in this land. For she knew that no power could silence or kill her true being. Sophia and Logos now understood that only by making their coming together could they show the true way to wholeness.

So Logos and Sophia became flesh together in the land and time of all created beings. They came as twin boy and girl to a couple in a small town in Africa. A bright star guided those with open eyes to come and see them.

Sophia and Logos grew as peacemakers, healers, and prophets. They amazed all who witnessed the miracles they performed. They taught and modeled partnership, holding all things in common. The human beings tried to separate them and even to turn them against each other. They tried to make Logos their ruler, but he refused to take any power over others. Then they thought they could appease him by offering to let Sophia be his assistant ruler, but Logos and Sophia refused. They would do nothing to destroy their equal relationship, and furthermore, they would not take any power over others.

After many years, the human beings began to recognize Sophia and Logos together as Messiah, divinely anointed to restore peace and wholeness to their land. The human beings began to worship Logos and Sophia as the Christ, the Messiah. The human beings repented of their violent ways and brought healing to their land. Once again they lived in loving partnership with one another, nurturing and respecting all other created beings. They sang hymns of praise to Sophia and Logos, their Christ. The divinely anointed Word of Wisdom became flesh in them, so that they could continue the work of creation.

Imagining Comings

Divide into small groups of four or five. Discuss the implications of the word "Advent," which means continual coming. Imagine other endings to the "Story of Comings." What other ways of restoring peace and wholeness to the land might Sophia and Logos have tried? Imagine other comings of the sacred. Each group might imagine an alternative ending to the story and then tell it to the larger community.

Hymn of Birthing   "O Christ-Sophia, Be Born in Us," #18

Imagining Birthings in our Lives

Each participant finds a comfortable place to sit or lie down. One person reads the following guided meditation.

Close your eyes and become aware of your breathing. Notice whether or not you are taking short, quick breaths or long, slow breaths. Now begin to control your breathing. Take a slow…and deep breath. Let your breath out slowly…and fully. Breathe in deeply…and slowly…through your nose. Breathe out slowly…and fully…through your mouth. Breathe in wholeness…deeply into your whole body-soul. Breathe out anything that would block wholeness in your life. Continue breathing in…slowly…and deeply…and breathing out…slowly…and fully.

As you continue breathing in…and breathing out…slowly…and deeply, imagine new possibilities for your life. Imagine yourself giving birth to something new…What is this new thing you are birthing? Is it a new idea or action or sacred experience or object you are creating? What do you need to do to give birth to this new thing? Imagine yourself in the perfect surroundings to give birth to this new thing. Imagine yourself taking all the steps necessary for the birthing. Now imagine yourself giving birth to this new something. Imagine your feelings as you give birth. Imagine others responding to your new creation in the ways that you desire them to respond.

As you continue breathing in…and breathing out….slowly…and deeply, imagine the difference your creation makes in the world. Imagine what you want to happen as a result of this new thing you have brought into the world. Imagine your feelings as you see changes taking place.

Slowly come back to this community and open your eyes, holding onto your feelings of giving birth.

Participants share their imagined birthings with the community, if they so desire.

Birthing Christ-Sophia

Voice 1   We come with individual experiences of giving birth.

Voice 2   We come with individual longings to give birth.

Voice 3   We come with different feelings about giving birth.

All   We all come together as a community to give birth to Christ-Sophia, sacred symbol of partnership, peace, and wholeness. We give birth to Christ-Sophia in many ways and through many experiences.

Voice 4   We give birth to Christ-Sophia by giving equal value to girls and boys of all races in our educational institutions.

Voice 5   We give birth to Christ-Sophia through sharing power in our workplace communities.

Voice 6   We give birth to Christ-Sophia through sharing our material possessions.

Voice 7   We give birth to Christ-Sophia through nurturing and respecting the earth and all created beings.

Voice 8   We give birth to Christ-Sophia by practicing mutuality in our personal relationships.

Voice 9   We give birth to Christ-Sophia by liberating ourselves and others from oppressive systems.

Voice 10   We give birth to Christ-Sophia through sharing power in our religious communities.

Voice 11   We give birth to Christ-Sophia through giving sacred value to female and male images in our worship experiences.

All   We are a community giving birth to Christ-Sophia. Through sharing power of leading and creating, we give birth to Christ-Sophia. Through naming the feminine and masculine divine in our worship, we give birth to Christ-Sophia. Through our words and actions Christ-Sophia is becoming flesh and living among us, full of grace and truth. We sing praise and glory to Christ-Sophia, who brings peace on earth, shalom to all creation.

Hymn of Fulfillment   "Christ-Sophia Now we Praise," #4

CELEBRATION OF WINTER SOLSTICE

Gather after dark at the time of the winter solstice. Sit in a circle or semicircle around a fire. On an altar beside the fire, place evergreen foliage and pictures or figurines of Black Madonnas or other black sacred images. Experience the service in the light of the fire alone. Have flashlights or candles available if some participants have trouble reading the liturgy in the firelight. Play soft music in the background.

Invoking Divine Darkness *(in unison)*

Holy Darkness, indwelling and surrounding us,
Dark Womb, who gives birth to all life,
we call upon your life-giving power.
As we celebrate winter solstice,
the darkest time of the year,
we praise you, O Divine Darkness,
who comes in many forms.

You come to us in figures
of Black Madonnas.
You come in the darkness
of Mother Earth.
You come in the image
of the dark Christ-Sophia.
You come to transform all life
in your cave of creativity.

We move with you into the great mystery
of the unknown, the uncontrolled, the unshaped.
O Holy Night, O Sacred Darkness,
we embrace you.

Reaffirmation of Darkness

Group 1   Darkness scares us because we cannot see what is out there. Darkness frightens us because it contains the unknown. We can be surprised in the darkness.

Group 2   Surprises excite us. We like the mystery that walks in darkness. We anticipate a new seeing in the midst of the unknown.

Group 1	In the darkness, we lack control. We don't know what's coming next. Darkness may hide our rational abilities.
Group 2	Darkness nourishes our creative abilities. Womb darkness sustains and nurtures us toward birth. Darkness is pregnant with new life.
Group 1	Darkness lowers our defenses. We cannot see to protect ourselves. Darkness feels chaotic and formless.
Group 2	Creation comes through darkness. Beauty is born in darkness. The Creative Spirit formed all life from darkness.
All	Darkness and light both come from the hand of the Creative Spirit, and they are good. We have failed to see the goodness in darkness because of our sin of racism and our fear of the unknown. We come now to reaffirm the goodness and the beauty and the creative power of darkness. In the beginning was darkness, the warm darkness of the creative Womb, and the darkness was good.

Original Blessing of Darkness

Reader 1	Originally, the darkness was blessed: "In the beginning God created the heavens and the earth. The earth was without form and void, and darkness was upon the face of the deep; and the Spirit of God was moving over the face of the waters" (Genesis 1:1–2 RSV). All life came forth from this darkness.
Reader 2	Darkness continues to be blessed by divine Presence: God speaks "with a loud voice...out of the fire, the cloud, and the thick darkness" (Deuternomy 5:22). Darkness surrounds deity as a "canopy" (2 Samuel 22:12). The Spirit gives us "the treasures of darkness and riches hidden in secret places" (Isaiah 45:3), so that we may experience sacredness.
All	We reaffirm the original blessing of darkness. We receive the treasures of darkness, and will search for the riches hidden in the dark places of our lives.

Blessing our Darkness

Participants take turns telling stories of darkness in their lives that brought some form of healing, transformation, creativity, and/or new life. After each story, the whole community gives the following response:

We bless the darkness within you.
We celebrate the darkness that transforms.
We praise the darkness
    that gives birth to new life.

One person reads the following poem as the others meditate silently.

Whittling at the Underlying
by Melanie Ferguson

The umbra is that
part of the shadow
cast by the moon,
in solar eclipse,
on the earth within which
the sun is totally hidden.

Melanie, the name, has always meant
some darkness. Darkness
may be a part of this name because,
before I could know it,
some things have always been
in shadow and not invited
to speak. And so on the
slow, sacred waves of time
comes the umbra.

In perfect
opposition, always
there are
and there
always
will be
tall lighthouses. On
shores that
you want
to reach.

On occasions,
in a circular row out, a white roar stretches out on the water, out into what is
your deepmoonlessness. And if you are patient to know what you
deeply mean in that non-light, the hope goddess will turn her head back around
at you, catch you in the strength of her long white arm, swing you around again
on the edge of darkness, onto a clairvoyant shore of long sailed for grace.

Hymn to Darkness   "O Holy Darkness, Loving Womb," #22

Celebration of Darkness

Participants say the following chant until all know it by memory:

> We bless the night and dance the dark;
>   to mystic lands we now embark.

Two people serve as the readers. All other participants speak the chant after each reading. As they chant, they hold hands and dance to the right on the first line and dance to the left on the second line.

Reader 1   Rejoice in the winter solstice!
Come celebrate the darkest time of year!
Praise the darkness at the center of the universe.
Embrace the darkness at the center of our beings.

All   We bless the night and dance the dark;
    to mystic lands we now embark.

Reader 2   The night brings us refreshing sleep
    and nurtures dreams from treasures deep.
Uncharted paths toward which we long
    become the theme of our night song.

All   We bless the night and dance the dark;
    to mystic lands we now embark.

Reader 2   The sensuous darkness of the night
    takes lovers to their greatest height.
The night restores with warm embrace
    and kisses us with healing grace.

All   We bless the night and dance the dark;
    to mystic lands we now embark.

Reader 2   Whispering souls in dark unite
    to share the secrets of the night.
Myths told in caves from age to age
    become the truth on sacred page.

All   We bless the night and dance the dark;
    to mystic lands we now embark.

Reader 2   The darkness of the womb gives birth
    to life and love throughout the earth.

From blackest soil comes richest fruit;
    the deepest night inspires the muse.

All   We bless the night and dance the dark;
    to mystic lands we now embark.

Reader 2   The darkness of the earth transforms
    the coldest death to living warmth.
Our healing comes when we let go
    and into darkness freely flow.

All   We bless the night and dance the dark;
    to mystic lands we now embark.

Reader 1   Come celebrate the darkness at the center:
    the generative darkness, the bounteous blackness,
    the fertile darkness, the luxurious blackness,
    the teeming darkness, the beautiful blackness.

All   We bless the night and dance the dark;
    to mystic lands we now embark.

Continue chanting the last two lines and dancing with the chant, going faster and faster and then slowing down to a stop.

Sending Forth into Darkness

Seated again around the fire, participants speak this benediction in unison.

We send one another forth into darkness,
    pregnant with new life, abundant with hope, filled with mystery.
We go forth with the dark Christ-Sophia,
    healing our wounds, transforming our fears, embracing the unknown.
We go forth into mystic lands
    where black and white, night and day, darkness and light,
    form one creative whole.

CELEBRATION OF EPIPHANY

As people gather, play music softly in the background. Form one large circle with an altar in the center. On the altar place one large candle in a holder, three containers with burning incense, and enough play dough for each participant to have a large piece.

Call to New Vision *(light candle on altar)*

Leader   The star leads us to new sights and new visions.

All   We come with open eyes and open minds.

Leader   "Ask, and it will be given you; seek and you will find" (Matthew 7:7 RSV).

All   We come asking and seeking.

Meditation on Epiphany

As one person reads the following meditation out loud, the others meditate silently.

Epiphany is the traditional Christian feast celebrating the manifestation of the divine nature of Jesus to the Gentiles, represented by the Magi. Almost two thousand years ago, Wisdom's children, called "Magi," received this new revelation of divinity.

The ruling powers of that day were not pleased by this revelation. King Herod did everything he could to squelch the revelation. Herod tried to trick the Magi into believing that he too was interested in new revelations. But they were wise enough to heed the warning they received in a dream telling them not to let Herod know the whereabouts of the divine child. Herod did not give up.

Those seeking to destroy new revelations can be tenacious and cruel. Herod ordered the killing of all the children in Bethlehem and the surrounding areas who were two years old or younger. The treacherous Herod thought he could thus destroy the new revelation that threatened his power.

But divine revelation could not be stifled. It was kept secure from the destroyers. An angel came to the divine child's parents in a dream, telling them to take the child far away from Herod's destructive power. Though the new revelation had to be hidden for awhile, it could not die.

Traditionally observed on January 6, Epiphany can occur anytime, anywhere. Epiphany is not limited to the experience of the Magi. "Epiphany" has come to mean "any revelatory manifestation of divine being." Revelations did not stop with the Magi. Epiphany continues to happen where minds and souls are open.

Manifestations of divinity come to us when we open our eyes widely enough. If we remove our blinders of fear and prejudice, new light will shine through. Revelatory manifestations of divinity surprise us with newness, just as the revelation of divine being lying in an animal feeding trough startled the Magi.

The fullness of divinity has long been hidden under layers of exclusively masculine sacred images. Feminine divine images may at first startle us with their unexpectedness. Because of our culture's long denigration of the feminine, we may even feel that feminine names are not lofty enough to carry divinity, just as the Magi must have at first wondered if divine revelation could come in the form of a small infant in a manger.

The early church believed that Jesus was a revelation of Sophia, or Wisdom. Early Christians associated Jewish wisdom literature's personified Sophia with Jesus. They saw Jesus as the incarnation of divine Sophia. But many Herods along the path of Christian history, in order to secure their own power, have tried to destroy the revelation of divine Sophia. Sophia has been hidden, but she could never die.

How would our society be different if Christ-Sophia had been recognized as a revelation of divinity? What new revelations of divinity have you experienced recently? Who or what has been your Herod seeking to destroy your revelation? Who or what has been your angel helping you guard your revelation from harm?

Each person takes a large piece of play dough to use in making visual images to represent their reflections upon the above questions. Each person will give shape to (1) divine revelations recently experienced, (2) would-be destroyers of their revelations, and (3) angel guardians of their revelations. Participants take turns telling the group the significance of the images they have created.

Community Covenant

Taking turns around the circle, each person holds the candle and says the following:

Revelations of divinity have come to me. (State specific revelations.) These epiphanies are sacred. Though some seek to destroy my revelations, they will never die. I will not let them die. Will you be my angels to help guard my revelations?

After each person speaks, the community responds in unison:

We covenant with you to be angel guardians of your sacred revelations. When forces seek to destroy your revelations, we will surround you with courage and support you with prayer. We will protect your revelations from harm. They will never die.

Standing and joining hands, the community speaks the following affirmation in unison:

Standing together we affirm the sacred power of our revelations. They will never die, but will live to bring healing and blessing to ourselves, to others, and to all creation. Our revelations come from the Divine Revealer. We will continue to open our minds and souls to new revelations. We stand together to guard one another's revelations from harm. In this community we will find courage and support to open our eyes wider to new truth and new visions from Christ-Sophia. We will open ourselves to epiphany.

Poem of Celebration *(stand and read in unison)*

Birth-Rebirth
by Barbara J. Middleton

She's here; She's finally here!
What was month by month, and day by day,
became hour by hour, minute by minute.

Her time…
Creation's time…
not dictated by schedule or whim.

Exhaustion, everyone's exhaustion,
from work well done, labor well laid:
a team, a community, a family;
part and particle of the universal family;
women and men laboring together
or alone but within the space
and time of NOW.

Even this day somewhere, somehow
the cries of birthing can be heard,
and in the cry is the sound of the
Spirit waiting for new life.
To continue what has been before
and will be again — LIFE.

Hymn of Celebration   "What Wondrous Thing," #36

Sending Forth to Epiphany (*stand and read in unison*)

We have sought and we have found.
We have looked and we have seen.
We go forth in the power
  of what we have seen and heard and felt.

Epiphany lights our way to new life.
Epiphany beckons us forward to new life.
We stand together on tiptoe,
  breathless for new discovery.

PALM SUNDAY CELEBRATION

Plan this service to be intergenerational. Before the service, ask participants to bring some object or symbol that has special significance to them and that they have never seen in a worship service before. Gather in a circle around an altar. Leave a space in the center of the altar. Around this space, place palm fronds, one for each child and adult.

Celebratory Hymn and Procession   "O Blessed Christ-Sophia," #17

As the adults sing the hymn, the children take palm fronds from the altar and wave them as they process around the room. They move around and in and out of the circle to the music. Then adults take palm fronds, waving them and processing with the children, while all sing the hymn again. After concluding, all place the palm fronds back on the altar, leaving a space in the center.

Call to Praise *(stand)*

Children	Come and see what is happening!
Adults	Calm down! We don't have time right now.
Children	But don't you hear all the shouts? Someone important is coming this way, and riding on a donkey.
Adults	Don't be ridiculous! No one important would ride on a donkey.
Children	Here they come. Just look and listen!
Adults	Well, what in heaven's name!
Children	Hosanna! Blessed is the One who comes riding on a donkey!
Adults	Who is it?
Children	Can't you see? It's Christ-Sophia, the wise and holy One.
All	Hosanna! Blessed is Christ-Sophia, the wise and holy One who comes riding on a donkey.

Seeing Holiness

Reader 1   Jesus sent two disciples, saying to them, "Go into the village ahead of you, and immediately you will find a donkey tied, and a colt with her; untie them and bring them to me'" (Matthew 21:1–2).

Reader 2   This took place to fulfill what had been spoken through the prophet, saying, "Tell the daughter of Zion, Look, your king is coming to you, humble, and mounted on a donkey, and on a colt, the foal of a donkey " (Matthew 21:4–5).

Reader 3   Sophia is bright, and does not grow dim. By those who love her she is readily seen, and found by those who look for her. Quick to anticipate those who desire her, she makes herself known to them. Watch for her early and you will have no trouble (Wisdom 6:12–14).

Reader 4   The crowds that went ahead of Jesus and that followed were shouting, "Hosanna to the Son of David! Blessed is the one who comes in the name of the Lord! Hosanna in the highest heaven!" (Matthew 21:9)

Reader 5   In each generation Sophia passes into holy souls, and she makes them friends of God and prophets…. She is indeed more splendid than the sun, she outshines all the constellations; compared with light, she takes first place (Wisdom 7:27, 29).

Offering of Sacred Symbols

Children take turns showing the objects or symbols they brought to the community, talking about their significance. After each finishes, he or she places the object in the center of the altar. Adults take turns showing the objects or symbols they brought to the community, talking about their significance and then placing them in the center of the altar. They might also comment on why they think these symbols have not been part of worship and their feelings about placing them on the altar. After all have finished, the whole community speaks the following response in unison:

> We offer these sacred symbols to Christ-Sophia,
>   the wise and holy One,
>   who comes in unexpected places
>   and surprising forms never seen before.
> Like mangers and donkeys and crosses,
>   our sacred symbols may seem unusual,
>   but they take their place on the holy altar.

Prayer of Confession *(in unison)*

> Christ-Sophia, you have come to children, women, and men down through the ages in many forms and through many names. You continually break out of our prescribed forms and surprise us with newness.

Forgive us for our blindness and our feeble attempts to limit you. As people long ago turned from shouts of "Hosanna" to cries of "Crucify," we also have been fickle in following you. We have rejected you when you have not fit our traditions and fulfilled our wishes.

Too long we have ignored and despised your feminine image and tried to contain you in masculine names. Even now, Christ-Sophia, as we speak your name, we confess our fear of the ridicule of those who do not understand, and the hostility of those who do understand the power of your name to bring change they do not want.

Forgive us and heal us of fear. Open our eyes to see you in unexpected forms. Amen.

Celebration of Surprise

Reader 1   From Sophia come all good things; from her hands come immeasurable riches (Wisdom 7:11).

Reader 2   In Christ all things in heaven and on earth were created, things visible and invisible (Colossians 1:16).

Reader 3   Christ-Sophia makes all things new (Wisdom 7:27, Revelation 21:5).

All   Christ-Sophia continually surprises us with good things.

The children name good surprises they have experienced. Then adults name good surprises they have experienced. As each surprise is named, the whole community responds with the following words, filling in the blank with the surprise named:

Christ-Sophia surprises us with (e.g., newborn kittens). Thanks be to Christ-Sophia.

Children   Surprises are so much fun! We love all the surprises of Christ-Sophia.

Adults   We celebrate the many surprises of Christ-Sophia. Our hearts rejoice in all these wonders.

All   Hosanna! Blessed is Christ-Sophia, the surprising One, who comes riding on a donkey.

Closing Hymn of Celebration   "O Blessed Christ-Sophia," #17

While singing this hymn, children and adults take palm fronds from the altar and wave them as they process together around the room. Children lead the procession, walking and dancing as they wish to the music.

EASTER COMMUNION CELEBRATION

Gather outside on Easter Sunday morning, if weather permits. If possible, pick a place with blossoming trees and flowers. Gather round a table on which are a chalice containing wine (or grape juice) and a freshly baked loaf of bread.

Seeking	(based on John 20:15; Matthew 25:35–37, 40; 1 Corinthians 1:24; Luke 4:18)
Reader 1	Whom do you seek?
Group 1	We seek Jesus who has risen from the dead! Do you know where we can find him?
Group 2	We want to find Jesus so that we can learn his secret of beating death.
Reader 2	Where are you seeking?
Group 1	We go to church every Sunday, and sing praises to Jesus, and give our tithes and offerings.
Group 2	We read our Bible and pray daily, and teach Sunday School, and serve on church committees.
Reader 1	Whom are you seeking?
Group 1	We told you we're seeking Jesus.
Group 2	We believe Jesus is the answer to all our problems.
Reader 2	Are you finding Jesus?
Group 1	Well, we're not so sure, because there's this longing deep down . . .
Group 2	Even when we're in church, we often feel empty and restless.
Reader 1	Whom are you seeking?
Reader 2	Where are you seeking?
Groups 1 & 2	Maybe that's our problem. Perhaps there's more to seeking.

Reader 1	Jesus said, "I was hungry and you gave me food, I was thirsty and you gave me something to drink, I was a stranger and you welcomed me, I was naked and you gave me clothing, I was sick and you took care of me, I was in prison and you visited me. As you did it to one of the least of these my brothers and sisters, you did it to me."
Groups 1 & 2	We have not sought Jesus among those people. It's hard to see Jesus in people like that.
Reader 2	The risen Christ is our wisdom, our Sophia. If we ask, we will receive the gift of Sophia, the wisdom to find Jesus in the faces of our hurting sisters and brothers. Christ-Sophia opens our eyes to see divinity in the face of the homeless man and the poor woman waiting in line for food.
All	Christ-Sophia, we come seeking you. We know this seeking will take us to difficult people and painful places. We trust that we will discover new life and new meaning as we find you in our needy sisters and brothers. O Risen Christ-Sophia, we seek to join you in bringing good news to the poor, proclaiming release to the captives, and letting the oppressed go free. Amen.

Hymn of Hope   "Love Rises Up," #15

Call to Resurrection

Voice 1	Up from the grave he arose!
Voice 2	What do you mean?
Voice 1	It's a line from an old gospel song.
Voice 2	But what does it mean?
Voice 1	It means that Christ rose from the dead.
Voice 3	And he lives today.
Voice 2	Where does he live today?
Voice 1	He lives in believers.
Voice 3	And in the community of believers.
Voice 2	So he lives in male believers and communities of men.

Voice 1	No, he lives in all believers and all communities.
Voice 2	Then why do you say "he"?
Voices 1 & 3	We never thought about it.
Group 1	We will begin to think about it, to bring the truth to light. The divine feminine has far too long been buried under the masculine.
Group 2	"Mother," "Daughter," "Sister," "Sophia"—"She" has been buried under "Father," "Son," "Brother," "Master,"—"He"; and we have all suffered.
Group 1	Through our hymns and litanies and sacred images, we have kept the Risen One entombed in masculinity. We have not experienced the fullness of the resurrection, and we have all suffered.
All	*(standing)* Up from the grave she arose! No longer is she buried, no more entombed. We proclaim her resurrection, as well as his resurrection! She arose to bring us all new life; sisters, brothers, women, men— all have new life and new possibilities because she arose from the dead. She continues to rise so that we may rise from the dead.

Each member of the community briefly tells an experience in which she or he has experienced new life, and then expresses a hope for resurrection in some area of his or her life.

| **All** | Christ-Sophia, our Sister and Brother, we claim your resurrection! May our hopes for new life take wing on your power and your wisdom. For we are your body, your life in our world today. Christ-Sophia, your life in us is our hope of glory. Amen. |

Song of Resurrection   "Rise Up, O Christ-Sophia," #26

Call to Celebration *(reading responsively)*

Reader 1	Come, let us celebrate the risen Christ-Sophia.
All	The One who came bringing Good News to the poor and setting the oppressed free rose from the dead and now lives within and among us all.
Reader 2	Let us celebrate the riches of the glory of this mystery, which is Christ-Sophia in us, the hope of glory (Colossians 1:27).

All	We celebrate the risen Christ-Sophia, the liberating, creative Spirit within each one of us.
Reader 3	Let us hear the voice of Christ-Sophia declaring, "As you did it to one of the least of these my brothers and sisters, you did it to me" (Matthew 25:40).
All	We hear Christ-Sophia calling us to minister to our needy brothers and sisters.
Reader 4	We are the body of the risen Christ-Sophia and individually members of it (1 Corinthians 12:27).
All	The risen Christ-Sophia lives as sisters and brothers gathered in loving community.
Reader 5	If Christ-Sophia has not been raised, then our faith has been in vain (I Corinthians 15:14).
All	Christ-Sophia has risen! Christ-Sophia lives today! Christ-Sophia lives within us. Christ-Sophia lives in our needy brothers and sisters around us. Christ-Sophia lives among us as we gather in community.

Call to Communion *(read responsively)*

Reader 1	Welcome to the joyful feast of the risen Christ-Sophia. Christ-Sophia now invites us to celebrate the feast of new life, saying, "Behold, I make all things new!" We come to eat the bread of life, the bread that is continually making us a new creation. We come to drink the cup of the new covenant, the covenant of grace and freedom. As we eat this bread and drink this cup, may we be empowered with new life and new freedom. Christ-Sophia is risen!
All	Christ-Sophia is risen indeed!
Reader 2	We are risen!
All	We are risen indeed!
Reader 3	So let us rejoice and give thanks!
All	Spirit of new life and freedom, Christ-Sophia, our risen liberator, we rejoice that you live within and among us. As we thrill to the beauty of freshly blossoming springtime, we celebrate your resurrection power in all creation. With great joy and gratitude, we gather as a community of

faith. As we come to feast on this bread and cup, open our eyes to new visions and new ways to make these visions reality. Amen.

Acts of Communion

Reader 3 takes the bread and chalice from the communion table and goes back to the circle, passing them to the person on her/his right with these words: "Eat the bread of new life"; "Drink the cup of the risen Christ-Sophia." Then that person passes the bread and chalice to the person on her/his right with the words of salutation, and so on around the circle.

Meaning of Communion *(in unison)*

Through eating this bread and drinking this cup, we proclaim the risen Christ-Sophia alive today. We proclaim Christ-Sophia alive in us. We proclaim Christ-Sophia alive in our community. We covenant with one another to minister to Christ-Sophia in our sisters and brothers living with poverty, violence, and injustice.

Through eating the bread and drinking the cup of the risen Christ-Sophia, we celebrate the divine feminine and the divine masculine. We celebrate our sacredness. We celebrate the sacredness of all creation.

Song of Celebration   "Christ-Sophia Lives Today," #2
Sing with hand movements.

EARTH DAY CELEBRATION

Plan this service to be intergenerational. Ask children and adults to bring newspapers, magazines, cans, and bottles for recycling. Bring empty egg and milk cartons for making decorations.

Gather outdoors on or near Earth Day, April 22. If possible, choose a place with lush foliage and blossoming flowers. Place a table in the center to serve as an altar. On the altar place bags for collecting paper, cans, and bottles for recycling. Also place scissors, paste, crayons, used magazines, recycled poster paper, pipe cleaners, and a shovel. In the center of the altar place a small tree to be planted by the community.

Hymn of Invocation   "Gather Us Under Your Warm Wings," #11

Call to Celebration of the Earth

Adult 1   Come, let us celebrate the wonders of Earth! Let us rejoice in the glory of each night and day; let us give praise for the abundance of Earth. Come, let us celebrate the life-giving Earth!

Child 1   Come laugh and sing and dance with joy;
     Earth delights each girl and boy.

All   We celebrate the lovely Earth;
     all forms of life she brings to birth.

Adult 2   We marvel at the amazing variety of plants and animals, the vastness of Earth's resources to sustain us all, the continual capacity of Earth to give birth to new life, our connection with all living beings.

Child 2   The Earth gives us good things to eat,
     and fresh, cool water in the heat.

All   We celebrate the lovely Earth;
     all forms of life she brings to birth.

Adult 3   Earth lavishes us with sensuous pleasures: iridescent flowers of sweetest scent, luscious fruits flowing with juice, gentle breezes whispering through stately trees.

Child 3   The Earth is filled with fun and glee,
     amazing sights for all to see.

All   We celebrate the lovely Earth;
     all forms of life she brings to birth.

Words of Sophia

Reader 1   All that is hidden, all that is plain, I have come to know, instructed by Wisdom (Sophia) who designed them all.... She deploys her strength from one end of the earth to the other, ordering all things for good (Wisdom 7:21, 8:1).

Reader 2   Hear the way of Sophia: "Go to the ant, you lazybones; consider its ways, and be wise. Without having any chief or officer or ruler, it prepares its food in summer, and gathers its sustenance in harvest" (Proverbs 4:11, 6:6–8).

Reader 3   The righteous know the needs of their animals, but the mercy of the wicked is cruel (Proverbs 12:10).

Reader 4   Sophia says, "And now, my children, listen to me: happy are those who keep my ways. Hear instruction and be wise, and do not neglect it. Happy is the one who listens to me, watching daily at my gates, waiting beside my doors. For whoever finds me finds life" (Proverbs 8:32–35).

Talk about the meaning of these words of Sophia. What do they have to say to us today about our care of creation? What new words do you believe Sophia is speaking to us today about caring for Earth?

Hymn of Confession   "O Mother Rock Who Bore Us, Unmindful We Have Been," #23

Commitment to Nurture the Earth

Children   Sophia tells us to take care of animals and plants. We promise to do all we can to care for animals and plants.

Adults   Sophia teaches us that Earth's resources are vast, but limited. We commit ourselves to conserve these resources.

Children   Other living beings have much to teach us. We promise to learn from other living beings.

Adults   From Sophia we discover our interdependence with all life. We vow to respect the value of other living beings.

Children   Sophia tells us that Earth is hurt and sick. We promise to do what we can to heal her.

Adults   Earth has become polluted with unhealthy waste products. We commit ourselves to do all we can to restore Earth.

Children   Earth's water, air, and land may not be safe when we grow up. We promise to do our part to clean up Earth.

Adults	We are passing down a dangerous environment to our children. We promise to do all we can to cleanse and nurture Earth.
All	Sophia teaches us to work together to make Earth well again. We promise to do our part for a healthy, beautiful Earth.

Children and adults bring waste newspapers, magazines, bottles, and cans and place them in the bags on the altar. All then work together to make Earth Day posters and banners. Create slogans, such as "Sophia says, Clean up Earth!" On the posters and banners, write the slogans, and draw pictures with crayons, or paste pictures from magazines. With the egg and milk cartons, make animal decorations to place on the altar. For example, a caterpillar can be made by cutting an egg carton in half, using pipe cleaners for legs and antennae, and coloring eyes and markings on the carton. Be creative!

An Earth Day Story

One of the children reads the following story to the community.

In New Mexico there lived a community of Native Americans called Navajos. The ancesters of the Navajos and other Native Americans were the first to live in America. These people loved the land and took good care of it. They called the Earth "our Mother." They believed that animals and people are the children of Earth. They believed that Earth took care of them and gave them everything they needed.

In return they were to take care of their Mother Earth. Because they truly appreciated all the gifts of Earth, they took only what they needed. Native Americans did not waste food, water, or trees. They did not believe that Earth belongs to people, but that people belong to Earth. They felt a spiritual presence in all things.

In the Navajo community in New Mexico there lived a sister and brother named Gaya and Henry Chee Clearwater. Gaya was twelve years old, and her brother Henry Chee was nine. They loved to play along the swift-running rivers and to drink from the clear blue lake in the center of their community. Playing hide and seek, they ran in and out of dark caves. While hiding in the caves, they loved to smell the damp dirt under their feet and to feel the smooth rocks surrounding them.

In springtime Henry Chee and Gaya picked purple and yellow wildflowers that grew along their pathway. Skipping and laughing with joy, Gaya wore the flowers in her hair. In the fall the children romped through the woods, crackling red and gold leaves beneath their feet. They helped their parents harvest ripened fruits and grains to store for the winter.

One day in early spring, when Earth was just beginning to wake from a deep sleep, Gaya and Henry Chee went out for a walk. They wanted to be the first to greet the new leaves budding on the trees and to welcome the pink flowers opening to the sun.

Henry Chee ran ahead of Gaya, yelling back, "Catch me, if you can!"

Gaya hollered, "I can and I will!"

Gaya ran as hard as she could and finally caught up with Henry Chee. Tired and thirsty, they collapsed by their favorite lake and leaned over to take a drink.

"Ugh!" exclaimed Henry Chee, spitting out the water. "This water tastes awful."

"It's worse than anything I ever tasted. And look! It's brown and grimy. What happened to the beautiful blue lake we loved so much?" asked Gaya.

"I don't know," said Henry Chee, "but I'm not drinking anymore."

"We must find out what happened," cried Gaya.

Sadly, Henry Chee and Gaya trudged home. They found their mother and father out in the field preparing the ground for the spring planting.

"Please come with us to the lake," Gaya said. "Something terrible has happened. The lake looks dingy, and the water tastes like…"

"Come on," Henry Chee blurted in; "an evil spirit has gotten into the water."

"We're busy now," said their father.

"We'll come later this evening," said their mother.

"No, you must come now," pleaded Gaya. "Something evil is going on."

Gaya and Henry Chee ran ahead of their father and mother to the lake. They took one look at the lake and knew that the children were right. Something terrible had happened. The clear blue lake had turned a murky grayish-brown color. Reluctantly, their mother and father stooped down and cupped their hands to hold a little of the lake water. They tasted only a sip, trying to determine what had gotten into the lake.

"I have no idea what has happened," said their father.

"Maybe we should go to the community meeting tomorrow evening and see if anyone knows about this," said their mother.

The next evening at the monthly community meeting, Mr. and Ms. Clearwater asked if anyone knew anything about the lake. Others at the meeting said that they had seen and tasted the change in the lake. But no one knew what had caused this change.

They all began to give their opinions about what had happened. Some thought that an evil spirit may have gotten into the lake. Others thought that some evil people outside their community had been jealous of their beautiful clear lake and had dumped some dirty materials in it. They all left the meeting not knowing how the lake had been polluted or what they were going to do about it.

Months passed. Spring turned into summer. The lake grew murkier. No one in the com-munity seemed to know what to do about it. Henry Chee and Gaya began to notice other things happening. The sunflowers that grew along the lake started wilting. Brown spots began to appear on the leaves of the giant oak trees near the lake.

On a hot day in mid-July, Henry Chee was walking alone through the woods near the lake. All of a sudden, he tripped over something. Taking one look, he screamed and ran home as fast as he could.

"Gaya, come see," he yelled between gasps. "Come see…it's so horrible! Come…help!"

Gaya ran with him to the clearing in the woods where he had tripped.

Looking down, she jumped back and screamed. There beneath her feet were several of the white and velvet green ducks that used to swim and play in the lake. They lay still on their backs—dead and rotting in the sun.

"That does it!" exclaimed Gaya. "I don't care what it takes! I'm going to find out what's going on here."

"I'll help you," said Henry Chee. "We've got to save our friends—the lake, the ducks, and the flowers."

Gaya and Henry Chee didn't tell their parents what they were going to do. They thought their mother and father would discourage them. After all, the adults in the community had decided there was nothing they could do about the lake. Henry Chee and Gaya determined that they would do something—no matter how long it took them.

In school Gaya had read some detective stories. Gaya and Henry Chee both watched mystery movies on television. They decided they could be detectives and find out who was destroying the lake. They first collected as much information as they could. Separately, they went to members of their community and asked questions. They asked people when they started noticing the lake changing colors, and if they had seen anyone they didn't know around the lake. Henry Chee and Gaya got a few clues that they followed. They found the addresses of the people outside the community who were seen around the lake. Then they sneaked away to find and question these people.

But after a month of searching and following all clues, Henry Chee and Gaya had still not solved the mystery of the lake. Maybe they should just quit. Summer was drawing to a close. When school started, they would have no time for their detective work.

The week before school started Gaya and Henry Chee went with their parents to the city close to their community. They were going to shop for school supplies and clothes. When they had gone about thirty miles outside their community, Gaya saw something she had never seen before—a large factory. Dingy grayish-brown smoke was coming from the factory.

Henry Chee noticed the factory too and said, "That smoke's the color of the lake."

Gaya replied, "That's exactly what I was thinking."

Their parents didn't see any connection. But Gaya decided that she had to go to the factory to see if it had caused the changes in the lake. She finally convinced her parents to stop by the factory on the way home. Gaya, Henry Chee, and their parents asked to speak to the supervisors of the factory. They asked the supervisors if they knew anything about the changes in the lake in their community.

The supervisors denied any knowledge of the lake. But the whole time they were in the factory, Henry Chee and Gaya smelled the same smell they had smelled in the lake. They could almost taste in the air of the factory that terrible taste that was in the lake water. By this time they had become good enough detectives that they knew the factory supervisors weren't telling the truth.

When they returned to school, Gaya and Henry Chee told their teachers what they believed was killing the lake. Some dirty waste products from the factory were somehow getting into the lake.

Because Henry Chee and Gaya presented such a good case, their teachers decided to see what they could discover. They went to the factory and found that Gaya and Henry Chee were onto something. The teachers called government officials to look into the matter.

The government workers responsible for protecting the environment came to examine the factory. They discovered that factory workers had been taking waste products and dumping them into the lake in the Navajo community at night, when they thought no one would see them. They did this so that they would not have to pay for safer ways to get rid of the waste. The waste products that were going out into the air through the factory's smoke were also hurting the lake and everything living around it.

The factory supervisors wanted to make more and more money. So they produced more products that made more waste. An evil spirit had gotten into the lake—the evil spirit of greed that led to the abuse of Earth. The government officials ordered the factory to stop dumping wastes in the lake, to pay to have the lake cleaned up, and to develop ways to keep waste products out of the air.

As fall breezes blew through the Navajo community, the lake again became crystal clear and sky blue. White ducks with velvet green heads again swam and played in the lake. Thirsty children paused from their play to drink the cool, clear water. The whole community rejoiced that the lake was restored to its original beauty. They held a great feast. School was dismissed for a whole day of celebration. The community danced and sang praises to Earth, their Mother.

Never before had they felt such appreciation for all her gifts, especially for the lake with its beautiful clear blue water. And never before had they been so grateful for bright children who love Earth and take good care of her.

At the celebration, the community gave special honor to Gaya and Henry Chee. They sat at the head of the banquet table. Members of the community listened intently as Henry Chee and Gaya told the story of how they solved the mystery of the lake. Gaya and Henry Chee received many gifts of appreciation. But the best gift of all was seeing the lake blue again and drinking its clean, refreshing waters.

Planting and Dedication of Tree

Participants take turns digging a hole for the tree. One adult begins by taking the shovel and loosening the dirt. Then a child shovels dirt out of the hole, followed by an adult who keeps shoveling. Continue rotating adult and child until all have taken a turn.

An adult and child together take the tree down from the altar and bring it to the hole. They place it in the ground and hold it while the other participants take turns shoveling the dirt around the tree until the hole is filled. Then the community speaks the following response in unison.

> We dedicate this tree
>   to the renewing of Earth.
> May it gladden the heart of Earth
>   as it brings beauty
>   and shade and fresh air.
>
> We promise to help Earth
>   nurture this tree as it grows to fullness.
> O Earth, may this tree be a tree of life
>   for all who come nearby.

Hymn to Earth   "We Give Thanks to You, Dear Earth," #33

CELEBRATION OF PENTECOST

Gather outside on or near Pentecost. Sit in a circle around a large table that will serve as an altar. On the table place fresh vegetables and flowers. Participants bring their best creations from the previous year or symbols of these creations. For example, if they have redecorated a room in their house, they can bring a sample of the wallpaper. If they have created a vegetable garden, they can bring the ripest vegetable from the garden. If they have written songs, they can bring their favorite.

Call to Celebration

Group 1   Come, let us celebrate the fruits of our labor.

Group 2   Let us celebrate the outpouring of the Spirit.

Group 1   We come bringing the best work of our hands.

Group 2   We come bringing the creations of our spirits.

Group 1   We celebrate the harvest of the Earth.

Group 2   We celebrate the coming of the Spirit.

Group 1   Pentecost celebrates the gifts of the Earth.

Group 2   Pentecost celebrates the gifts of the Spirit.

All   Pentecost brings Earth and Spirit together in celebration and blessing. First fruits of harvest, rushing wind, and tongues of fire—all are miracles, merging Earth and Spirit.

Group 1   We come expecting new blessings from Earth and Spirit.

Group 2   We come open to the miracles of Earth and Spirit.

All   Earth and Spirit, fill us with your miraculous blessings, as we open ourselves to you.

Hymn of Celebration   "Come, Thou From Whom All Blessings Flow," #8

Meditation on Pentecost

One person reads this meditation to the community.

Pentecost began as an ancient Hebrew harvest festival. In the Hebrew Scriptures, the name for this observance is *Shavuot,* or "Feast of Weeks." Celebrated fifty days after Passover, this important Jewish holiday was an agricultural festival affirming God's ownership of the land and thanking God for its fruitfulness. It is also called the "festival of harvest": "You shall observe the festival of harvest, of the first fruits of your labor, of what you sow in the field. You shall observe the festival of in-gathering at the end of the year, when you gather in from the field the fruit of your labor" (Exodus 23:16). For this celebration, the people were to bring the "choicest of the first fruits" of the ground to God (Exodus 23:19).

In the Hellenistic period, Pentecost began to lose its association with agriculture and came to be associated with the religious history of the Hebrew people. After 70 A.D., Pentecost became an observance of the giving of Torah on Mount Sinai. The interval between Passover and the arrival at Sinai was fifty days, according to an interpretation of Exodus 19:1. The term "Pentecost," from a Greek word meaning "fiftieth," thus continued to designate this observance.

In the first century, Pentecost became an observance in the Christian tradition. The second chapter of Acts records the first Pentecost after the death and resurrection of Jesus. In this passage, the apostles and others had gathered in Jerusalem on the day of Pentecost: "And suddenly from heaven there came a sound like the rush of a violent wind, and it filled the entire house where they were sitting. Divided tongues, as of fire, appeared among them, and a tongue rested on each of them. All of them were filled with the Holy Spirit and began to speak in other languages, as the Spirit gave them ability" (Acts 2:2–4).

The apostle Peter interpreted this event as the fulfillment of the prophecy of Joel (Acts 2:14–21). Within the context of the book of Acts, the events associated with Pentecost also fulfill the promise of the risen Christ, who had said, "You shall receive power when the Holy Spirit has come upon you" (Acts 1:8). Thus the Christian tradition celebrates Pentecost as the coming of the Holy Spirit, giving birth to the church.

The significance of Pentecost as a celebration of "first fruits" continued into the early Christian movement. The apostle Paul appears to have the original observance in mind when he says, "If the part of the dough offered as first fruits is holy, then the whole batch is holy; and if the root is holy, then the branches also are holy" (Romans 11:16).

We can enrich our Pentecost celebrations by reclaiming its original significance and combining it with its later meanings. A spiritual celebration of harvest helps us to see the sacredness of Earth and all her fruits. Observing the giving of Torah celebrates the sacred gift of order. Celebrating the outpouring of the Spirit opens possibilities for the miraculous to enter all of life. Pentecost then brings Earth and Spirit together, celebrating sacred gifts.

Blessing of First Fruits

Members take turns coming to the altar with their best creations from the previous year or symbols of these creations. They give a brief description of the importance of this creation to them, and then place it on the altar. (If the creation is something they have written, they may choose to read it or sing it.) After each one has finished, the group responds with the following words:

> Blessed be the work of your hands.
> Blessed be the fruit of your spirit.
> Your creation comes from the Creator
> of all good gifts of Earth and Spirit.

Claiming Pentecostal Power

Voice 1 "Earth's crammed with heaven and every common bush afire with God; those who see take off their shoes. The rest sit around it and pluck black-berries."[22]

All What did you say?

Voice 1 Those are lines from a poem by Elizabeth Barrett Browning. They illuminate the meaning of Pentecost.

Voice 2 Pentecost opens our eyes to see holiness all around us, in the beauty of the Earth aflame with the Spirit.

Voice 3 Pentecost opens our souls to reverence the holy beauty in Earth and in every living being.

All Too long we have failed to notice. We have walked by fields of splendor with shoes on and hands greedy for our own gain.

Voice 1 Now is the time to take off our shoes, for we stand on holy ground every day.

Voice 2 Today is the day to lift our hands in praise for bushes burning at our backdoor.

Voice 3 Now is the time to open our hearts to the fiery passion of the creative Spirit.

All We claim Pentecostal power—lavish like harvest of first fruits, rushing like mighty winds, burning like tongues of fire—energizing our body-souls. Empowered with Pentecost, we plant a new crop, sing a new song, speak a new language, create a new way.

Going Forth with Pentecostal Power *(in unison)*

Spirit infusing the Earth with glory and majesty,
   flowing in and out, surrounding and filling,
   living in all, and more than all,
   send us forth in your power.

Spirit in Earth and Earth in Spirit,
   fill us with your creative energy.
May we go forth rejoicing in your gifts,
   blessed in our work,
   and ripe for your full harvest in us.

CELEBRATION OF SUMMER SOLSTICE

Gather outdoors at the time of the summer solstice. Choose a place surrounded by trees and vegetation. Come together a little before sunrise. Sit quietly in a circle and meditate with soft music in the background. As the sun rises, begin the ritual.

Invoking the Sun *(all standing)*

>Life-giving Sun, we rise to greet you
>>on this longest day of the year,
>>when we see you in your fullest glory.
>
>We celebrate your power
>>to nurture us and all living beings
>>with your warmth and light.
>
>O Sun, who rises without our bidding,
>>we call on you to awaken us
>>to your miraculous life.
>
>With your energy
>>birds soar through lustrous skies,
>>fish swim in glistening streams,
>>flowers blossom in brilliant hues,
>>children grow in height and joy.
>
>By your light beauty springs forth
>>throughout land and sky and sea.
>
>With the rhythm of your rising
>>and setting comes the miracle of life.

Dance of Celebration

Form two groups. One group joins hands and moves in a circle around another group, as the group in the center of the circle speaks the following chant four or five times, growing faster and louder with each time.

>All of life is miracle;
>Each day brings wonders new.
>With dancing of the earth and sun,
>>whole worlds come into view.

The two groups now exchange places. The group in the center of the circle speaks the above chant four or five times, growing faster and louder with each time, while the group forming the circle moves around them.

Then the group in the center joins hands with the other group, forming a large circle. All move together in a large circle, several times to the right and then several times to the left, while speaking the above chant.

Hymn of Celebration   "New Miracles Unfold," #16

Dialogue on Miracles

Speaker 1   A miracle is anything that cannot be explained by the laws of nature. Many things that once were considered miracles, like the sun's rising, can now be explained in scientific terms.

Speaker 2   Even those things that science can explain still seem miraculous to me. Science tells us that we perceive the sun to rise because of the earth's rotation. But how did our solar system come into being in the first place, and what keeps it in motion?

Speaker 1   The Hubble space telescope out beyond the earth's atmosphere is providing new scientific data about the origin of the universe. It is revealing that there are other planets in other solar systems that may sustain life. This knowledge stretches our minds, but it is all part of the natural world. Science will one day be able to explain other things that seem miraculous to us today.

Speaker 2   Scientific knowledge about the origin and vastness of the universe makes it no less miraculous to me. Biological science can classify the systems in our bodies and explain how these systems function together. But the more I learn about human life, the more miraculous it seems. The more I experience of illness and healing, the more I believe that health is a miracle.

Speaker 1   Health certainly depends upon more than just physical processes. Scientific studies are discovering the connection of body, mind, and spirit.

Speaker 2   Even if scientific studies can verify the relationship between our physical and spiritual well-being, it still seems miraculous to me. I don't know that anyone will ever be able to give a scientific explanation for feelings like love. It's a miracle that we are emotional and spiritual beings.

Speaker 1   That is all part of our nature as human beings. My definition of "miracle" is an event beyond the laws of nature; it is a supernatural event. Many such events are recorded in the Bible. Miracles still occur today, but not frequently.

Speaker 2   The natural, as well as the supernatural, is included in my definition of "miracle." To me the natural world—the earth and all living beings—is miraculous. Anything that excites awe and wonder is a miracle to me. The beauty of nature excites my awe. Relationships and events in my life excite my wonder. Life itself is a miracle.

Open this discussion to all participants. Each participant, who so desires, gives her or his definition of "miracle."

Stories of Miracles

Reader 1   The mighty one. . . speaks and summons the earth from the rising of the sun to its setting (Psalm 50:1).

Reader 2   I will remember your wonders of old. I will meditate on all your work, and muse on your mighty deeds (Psalm 77:11b–12).

Reader 3   You do great things beyond understanding, and marvelous things without number (Job 9:10).

Use the following personal story of the author in any way that will stimulate participants to tell their stories of miracles.

"A Catholic press publishing feminist theology written by an ordained Baptist woman—now that's a miracle!" said a friend. I started into an explanation and stopped short. She was right. That was a miracle.

After writing a feminist christology, I knew that the hard part had just begun. Finding the right publisher to get the book to the intended audience posed an even bigger challenge. My work was too liberal for the majority of religious publishers and too conservative for many publishers of feminist books. In addition, the purpose of my book was to provide a bridge between academic feminist theology and laypeople in the pews. Since it contained both theological theory and rituals, it was not easy to classify. I wondered if it would fit the publishing needs of either academic or lay religious presses.

As I was putting the finishing touches on my manuscript, the name of a publisher came across my desk. I was going through copyright permission statements I had secured for some of the worship resources in my book. Twenty-Third Publications in Mystic, Connecticut, had given me permission to use a prayer. I liked the name of the company and especially the name of its location—Mystic.

When I looked up information about this publishing company and discovered it was Catholic, I hesitated. Although the leading feminist theologians were Catholic, I doubted that the majority of Catholic publishers were receptive to their works. Twenty-Third was probably a traditional Catholic press that would be no more open to my feminist christology than a Baptist press.

Nevertheless, I felt drawn toward Twenty-

Third Publications. I mailed the manuscript to Mystic.

Within two weeks, the editor called me, expressing interest in publishing my book. A month later, I had a contract with Twenty-Third to publish the book the next fall. I had wanted the book to come out as soon as possible after the 1993 "Re-Imagining Conference," which stirred controversy over the use of feminine sacred images, especially that of Sophia.

One of the purposes of my book was to give sound biblical and theological support for using the symbol of Sophia in worship. My goal was to have the book published by the end of 1995. I thought it would be a miracle if it came out any sooner. The miracle happened. *In Search of the Christ-Sophia: An Inclusive Christology for Liberating Christians* was published in the fall of 1994.

The miracle did not stop with the publication of the book. Almost immediately, a group of people from various denominations began meeting in a Baptist church to practice feminist christology. In the spring of 1995 a woman from the Russian Orthodox tradition, doing research for a paper to present at the September, 1995 NGO Forum on Women in Beijing, China, discovered *In Search of the Christ-Sophia* in a local bookstore. After many phone calls, she connected with me and the feminist worship group. Since then, she has been one of the most faithful, creative members of the community. This community, now called New Wineskins, has given birth to another community in a neighboring city.

The book has also connected me with some amazing Catholic women who have begun the New Creation Ministry in Nacogdoches, Texas. Reviews in the *Re-Imagining Newsletter, The Catholic Times, Catholic Women's Network,* and *Baptist Peacemaker* have also convinced me of the timeliness of the book's publication and the rightness of the publisher.

With the encouragement of Twenty-Third Publications and the New Wineskins Community, my writing has taken a new and unexpected turn. From my graduate school and college teaching experience, I had become quite comfortable with scholarly writing. Serving as a pastor in a local church and in a hospital setting gave me experience in translating academic theology into lay language. Most of my writing has been intended to persuade laypeople through rational argument. But I came to see that people's objections to feminine images in worship go deeper than the rational level. The emotional and spiritual levels can only be reached through the language of poetry and hymns and parables.

The more I explored the image of Christ-Sophia for my own emotional and spiritual life, the more my writing changed. The creative process became more fascinating and fun than ever before. Beginning with a new text to a familiar Christmas carol, I began writing hymns to Christ-Sophia.

From somewhere deep within my spirit these hymns kept coming. Hymns had been vital to my faith development as I grew up in a Baptist church and family who loved music. My spiritual journey with Christ-Sophia thus led me to creating hymns.

Beginning with a new image and a familiar tune from my childhood, a line would come and then a stanza and then another. Sometimes lines would come through my dreams. The pain of exclusion, felt unconsciously and consciously for so many years, slowly began to heal with the writing and singing of these new hymns. When I saw tears roll down the cheeks of members of the New Wineskins Community as we sang these hymns to Christ-Sophia, I knew that we were singing ourselves back into reality and power. We were experiencing healing at the deepest levels of our beings.

And so my writing continued from a place beyond reason. The journey of faith with Christ-Sophia freed me to take risks. Poems and stories and liturgies came from new feelings of creative freedom. This greater freedom did not eliminate the struggle, however.

The writing process became more demanding as more and more options opened before me. It took faith to try new forms. It took faith to continue working on pieces that required a long time to develop. I learned that the more faith I had in the Creative Spirit within me, the more freedom I discovered in the creative process. Beginning was always the hardest part. Once begun, the piece took on a life of its own, and I tried to stay within its flow.

The creative process feels like a miracle to me. I cannot explain it. I cannot predict it or program it. I must simply believe in it and be present with it. The creative process goes beyond my understanding and power, yet demands my fullest understanding and power. It excites my awe and wonder. The miracle of creativity happens for me in partnership with Christ-Sophia.

Invite members of the group to tell their stories of miracles.

Doxology   "Come, Thou From Whom All Blessings Flow," #8

INDEPENDENCE DAY

Before the service, ask participants to bring two symbolic objects: one symbolizing an area of their lives in which they experience bondage and the other symbolizing an area in which they experience freedom.

Gather outdoors in the late afternoon. Sit in a circle around a table. Place a large trash can beside the table. On the table, place firework sparklers (at least three for each participant) and matches. (If the meeting is in a place where fireworks are illegal, substitute small candles.)

Call to Freedom

Group 1 "Mine eyes have seen the glory."

Group 2 What are you talking about?

Group 1 That's a line from a patriotic hymn, and this is the 4th of July.

Group 2 We know, but that hymn glorifies victory through military might.

Group 1 That's true, but today we can see a different kind of glory.

Group 2 We see the glory of a peace and justice beyond anything Julia Ward Howe could have imagined when she wrote that hymn.

Group 1 Yes, that's the glory we can celebrate today!

Group 2 But we still have such a long way to go, even in our own "sweet land of liberty."

Group 1 Is there true liberty in a land where the majority of the poor are women and children?

Group 2 Can there be peace in a land where people of color earn far less than their white brothers and sisters?

Group 1 Is there liberty in a land where so many women are sexually harassed on the job and battered in their own homes?

Group 2 Can there be justice in a land where minorities and women of all colors continue to suffer from abuse and discrimination in the marketplace and even in church?

Group 1 How can we sing of glory and freedom when so many people are still in bondage?

Group 2 We sing and speak of a better land.

Group 1 We join in the call for freedom and justice for all.

Group 2	We will speak our visions of a place where we can all be free at last.
Group 1	Our words carry great power to create and define reality.
Group 2	Words carry power to redeem the brokenness caused by prejudice, injustice, violence, and discrimination.
Group 1	Words carry power to heal our broken land.
Group 2	We will speak our visions into reality.
Group 1	We will sing our visions into reality.
Group 2	We will act our visions into reality.
Group 1	We will dance our visions into reality.
Group 2	Let us begin by joining together in speaking our vision, in sounding our call to freedom.
All	We envision a land where the truth that all people are created equal will become a reality. Our vision is of a land where "liberty and justice" for all is more than a pledge. Our vision is of a land where women and men of all colors will share equally in opportunities and blessings.
	We envision an end to war not only across the seas but in our own city streets, an end to abuse of all kinds on the job and in the home. Our vision includes faith communities in which women and men of all colors share equally in leadership and ministry, communities which give sacred value to feminine divinity as well as to masculine divinity.
	We envision a land free of discrimination and injustice in any form. We sound a call to freedom in our institutions and in our homes. We call for individual freedom from external definition, freedom to follow the voice within. We call for freedom to love, to create, to laugh, to learn, to grow, to become all we are meant to be.

Song of Freedom *(all stand)*   "We Sound a Call to Freedom," #34

Words of Freedom

Reader 1	Is not this the fast that I choose: to loose the bonds of injustice, to undo the thongs of the yoke, to let the oppressed go free, and to break every yoke? Is it not to share your bread with the hungry, and bring the homeless poor into your house; when you see the naked, to cover them, and not to hide yourself from your own kin? Then your light shall break forth like the dawn, and your healing shall spring up quickly (Isaiah 58:6–8).
Reader 2	The Spirit…is upon me, because she has anointed me to bring good

news to the poor. She has sent me to proclaim release to the captives and recovery of sight to the blind, to let the oppressed go free (Luke 4:18).

Reader 3   Christ-Sophia says, "If you continue in my word, you are truly my disciples; and you will know the truth, and the truth will make you free" (John 8:31–32).

Reader 4   If Christ-Sophia makes you free, you will be free indeed (John 8:36).

Reader 5   For the law of the Spirit of life in Christ-Sophia has set you free from the law of sin and of death (Romans 8:2).

Reader 6   For freedom Christ-Sophia has set us free. Stand firm, therefore, and do not submit again to a yoke of slavery (Galatians 5:1).

Reader 7   There is no longer Jew or Greek, there is no longer slave or free, there is no longer male or female; for all of you are one in Christ-Sophia (Galatians 3:28).

Reader 8   Get wisdom; get insight; do not forget, nor turn away from the words of my mouth. Do not forsake her, and she will keep you; love her, and she will guard you.... Prize her highly, and she will exalt you; she will honor you if you embrace her. She will place on your head a fair garland; she will bestow on you a beautiful crown (Proverbs 4:5–6, 8).

Acts of Freedom

Participants take turns placing on the table symbols of areas in their lives in which they experience bondage. As they do so, they share what they wish about their feelings of pain and struggle. After each person speaks, the group responds with the following words of covenant:

> We hear your words of struggle as you strive to free yourself from bondage. We pledge to you our support on this important path. Make gaining your freedom the first priority in your life. Your freedom is vital to the fulfillment of your creative potential. Christ-Sophia has made you free; therefore cast off everything that binds you. Claim your freedom.

After hearing these words, the person lights a sparkler (or candle), takes the sparkler in one hand and the symbolic object in the other, and makes circular motions with the sparkler around the object. Then the person chooses one of the following acts (depending on the object and its symbolism): (1) throws the object in the trash can; (2) lights another sparkler and burns the object. After performing this act, the person speaks the following words:

> With this act, I claim my freedom. The sacred fire lights and empowers my path to freedom. I choose to cast off that which binds me.

Participants take turns placing on the table symbols of areas in their lives in which they experience freedom. As they do so, they talk about this experience of freedom and their feelings about it. If they have just recently gained freedom in this area, they may wish to tell about their struggle to gain independence. After each person speaks, the group responds with the following words of affirmation:

> You have listened to the truth of the Spirit within you, and you have experienced freedom. You have claimed the power of your inner wisdom. Christ-Sophia has made you free indeed. Hold on to your freedom and never submit to bondage of any kind. Freedom is your blessing and your calling. Continue to claim your freedom as you grow in love and creativity.

After hearing these words, the person lights a sparkler (or candle) and makes circular motions around herself or himself. Then the person walks, skips, or dances around the whole circle, twirling the sparkler. After performing this act, the person speaks the following words:

> Freedom's sacred fire surrounds me and empowers me. For freedom I was created. Freedom calls me on to new discoveries.

Dance of Freedom

All participants stand in a circle, holding sparklers (or candles). The circle should be large enough so that each person has plenty of room to move his or her arms in wide motions. One person lights a sparkler and with it lights the sparkler of the person on her or his left. That person does the same, and so on around the circle until every sparkler is lighted.

While singing the refrain of "We Sound a Call to Freedom," #34, all swing sparklers in circular motions. Then while singing the chorus again, several people stand in the center of the circle twirling sparklers and the others move around the circle in time with the music.

> Free at last, O Hallelujah!
> Free at last, O Hallelujah!
> Christ-Sophia, you have freed us!
> Your truth has set us free.

Sending Forth in Freedom *(in unison)*

> We feel the fresh air of freedom
>   filling us with joy and energy.
> Christ-Sophia has set us free,
>   and we are free indeed!
> We are free to love, to laugh, to dance, to sing,
>   to create a land where all can be free.
> We now go forth filled with freedom's breath,
>   inspired with freedom's fire,
>   singing freedom's song.

ENDNOTES

1. Jeanne Achterberg, *Woman as Healer* (Boston: Shambhala, 1990), p. 3.

2. Riane Eisler, *The Chalice and the Blade* (San Francisco: HarperCollins, 1987), pp. 29-43. See Eisler's description of Cretan civilization from around 6000 to 2000 B.C.E. The goddess-worshipping Cretans gave highest value to the generative, nurturing, and creative powers. The culture was marked by harmony and partnership between women and men, equitable sharing of wealth, artistic creativity, love of beauty and nature, and love of peace. See also Merlin Stone, *When God was a Woman* (New York: Harcourt Brace Jovanovich, 1976).

3. Elisabeth Schüssler Fiorenza, *In Memory of Her* (New York: Crossroad, 1989), p. 135.

4. Caitlin Matthews, *Sophia, Goddess of Wisdom: The Divine Feminine from Black Goddess to World-Soul* (London: Mandala, 1991), pp. 11-96.

5. Sergei Bulgakov, *Sophia: The Wisdom of God* (New York: Lindisfarne Press, 1993), p. 5.

6. Mary Kathleen Speegle Schmitt, *Seasons of the Feminine Divine, Cycle C: Christian Feminist Prayers for the Liturgical Cycle* (New York: Crossroad, 1994), pp.18-19.

7. U.S. Bureau of the Census, *Statistical Abstract of the United States: 1995* (115th edition.) Washington, DC, 1995, p. 480. Arloc Sherman, *Wasting America's Future: The Children's Defense Fund Report on the Costs of Child Poverty* (Boston: Beacon Press, 1994), p. xvi.

8. United Nations World Food Council, *Hunger and Malnutrition in the World: Situation and Outlook, 1991 Report* (New York: World Food Council, 1991), p. 5.

9. *Our Words, Our Voices: Young Women for Change! A report from the project "A Young Women's Portrait Beyond Beijing '95,"* sponsored by UNFPA and UNICEF, p. 49.

10. *Our Words, Our Voices*, p. 49. Paul R. Dekar, "And a Little Child Shall Lead Them" *Seeds* 17 (September, 1995), pp. 15-18.

11. *New York Times* (August 20, 1995), Sec. 3, p. 2.

12. "CQ Guide to Current American Government," *Congressional Quarterly* (Spring, 1995), p. 59.

13. Julian of Norwich, *Revelations of Divine Love*, ed. Dom Roger Hudleston (London: Burns & Oates, 1927), p. 119.

14. Quoted in Jacqueline Bernard, *Journey Toward Freedom: The Story of Sojourner Truth* (New York: W.W. Norton and Company, 1967), p. 150.

15. Sojourner Truth, "'Ar'n't I a Woman' Speech," in *Narrative of Sojourner Truth*, ed. Margaret Washington (New York: Vintage Books, 1993), p. 118.

16. Susan B. Anthony, "Constitutional Argument," in *Elizabeth Cady Stanton/Susan B. Anthony: Correspondence, Writings, Speeches*, ed. Ellen Carol DuBois (New York: Schocken Books, 1981), p. 154.

17. Quoted in Judith Bentley, *Harriet Tubman* (New York: Franklin Watts, 1990), p. 46.

18. Meister Eckhart, "Commentary on Genesis," in *Meister Eckhart: The Essential Sermons, Commentaries, Treatises, and Defense*, trans. Edmund Colledge and Bernard McGinn (New York: Paulist Press, 1981), p. 90.

19. St. John of the Cross, "Dark Night," in *St. John of the Cross: Alchemist of the Soul: His Life, His Poetry, His Prose*, ed. and trans. Antonio T. de Nicolás (New York: Paragon House, 1989), p. 103.

20. John Stuart Mill, "The Subjection of Women," in *Essays on Sex Equality*, ed. Alice S. Rossi (Chicago: University of Chicago Press, 1970), p. 125.

21. Martin Luther King, Jr., "I Have A Dream," in *A Testament of Hope: The Essential Writings of Martin Luther King, Jr.*, ed. James Melvin Washington (San Francisco: Harper & Row, 1986), p. 219.

22. Elizabeth Barrett Browning, "Aurora Leigh," Seventh Book, lines 821-825, in *The Poetical Works of Elizabeth Barrett Browning* (Boston: Houghton Mifflin, 1974), p. 372.

HYMNS

1 CELEBRATE A NEW DAY DAWNING

(Isaiah 55:12)

1. Cel - e - brate a new day dawn - ing, sun - rise of a gold - en morn;
2. Christ - So - phi - a lights the path - way to a world of har - mo - ny;
3. Sing a song of ju - bi - la - tion, dance with joy - ous rev - el - ry;

1. Christ - So - phi - a dwells a - mong us, glo - rious vi - sions now are born.
2. Sis - ter - Bro - ther Love sur - rounds us, nour - ish - ing our syn - er - gy.
3. Clap - ping trees and laugh - ing riv - ers join our call to lib - er - ty.

1. E - qual part - ners 'round the ta - ble, we make dreams re - al - i - ty;
2. Earth joins in our rich com - mun - ion, grate - ful for our heal - ing care;
3. Free at last to blos - som ful - ly, flow'r - ing forth in beau - ty bright,

1. Call - ing out our gifts we nur - ture hope be - yond all we can see.
2. Leap - ing deer and soar - ing ea - gles, all Earth's full - ness now can share.
3. We be - come a new cre - a - tion, burst - ing o - pen in - to light.

Words © 1996 Jann Aldredge-Clanton

HYMN TO JOY Ludwig van Beethoven, 1770–1827; adapted Edward Hodges 1796–1867

116

1. Christ - So - phi - a lives to - day, Al - le - lu - ia!
2. Sing we now this bless - ed morn Al - le - lu - ia!
3. Cel - e - brate a bright new life, Al - le - lu - ia!
4. Christ - So - phi - a ris - es glo-rious, Al - le - lu - ia!

1. Show-ing us the truth, the way, Al - le - lu - ia!
2. Christ-So - phi - a's work is born, Al - le - lu - ia!
3. Christ-So - phi - a ends the strife, Al - le - lu - ia!
4. All cre - a - tion sings vic - to-rious, Al - le - lu - ia!

1. Free at last, we all can be, Al - le - lu - ia!
2. Wis - dom, jus - tice, lib - er - ty, Al - le - lu - ia!
3. Sound the news to eve - ry land, Al - le - lu - ia!
4. Hope springs forth, sur - prise a - bounds, Al - le - lu - ia!

1. Make the vi - sion plain to see, Al - le - lu - ia!
2. Come cre - ate the ju - bi - lee, Al - le - lu - ia!
3. Join to - geth - er hand in hand, Al - le - lu - ia!
4. Earth trans-formed with joy re - sounds, Al - le - lu - ia!

EASTER HYMN *Lyra Davidica*, 1708;
adapted from *The Compleat Psalmodist*, 1749

3 CHRIST-SOPHIA NOW WE BLESS

(Psalm 104)

1. Christ - So - phi - a now we bless; Songs of joy our thanks pro-fess.
2. Christ - So - phi - a comes in light, Touch-ing earth with beau-ty bright;
3. Christ - So - phi - a fills the earth With a - bun - dant love and mirth.
4. Christ - So - phi - a stirs our hearts With a vi - sion to im-part,

1. We re - joice in eve - ry grace, Beau-ty glow-ing in each face,
2. Val - leys gush forth crys - tal streams; Rock-y can - yons blush with dreams;
3. Char - iot clouds on an - gel wings, Glad-ness to all hearts they bring.
4. All cre - a - tion fed and full, Freed from eve-ry sti - fling rule,

1. Fra - grant flow'rs and gold - en grain, Sing-ing birds, re - fresh-ing rain;
2. Graz - ing cat - tle, moun-tain goats, Friend-ly squirrels and spright-ly colts,
3. Car - ing friends who gath - er near Share our laugh-ter, hopes and tears.
4. Men and wom - en shar - ing pow'r, Part-ners for all gifts to flow'r.

1. All these gifts our souls in - spire, Light-ing our cre - a - tive fire.
2. Liv - ing be - ings great and small, Wis - dom made and keeps them all.
3. For these gifts so rich and free, May we ev - er grate-ful be.
4. For this world our spir - its pray; Christ - So - phi - a lights the way.

Words © 1996 Jann Aldredge-Clanton   ST. GEORGE'S WINDSOR George J. Elvey, 1816–1893

118

CHRIST-SOPHIA NOW WE PRAISE 4

1. Christ - So- phi - a now we praise; Joy - ful songs our voic- es raise.
2. Praise the glo- rious Queen of Wis-dom; Praise the Ev - er - last - ing One.
3. Christ - So- phi - a is the way, Truth, and life for us to - day.

1. For new life in us to birth, For deep heal - ing of the earth.
2. Life and hope to all she brings; Pris - on doors wide o - pen flings.
3. By her Spir - it in us all, We take up the jus - tice call.

1. Long her face we did not see; Blind no more our eyes shall be.
2. Lib - er - ty is ours to claim, By the pow - er of her name.
3. Fear not, she will give us cour-age To make peace, all be - ings nour-ish.

1. Long we've need-ed her em - brace, Glo - ry and pow - er of her grace.
2. Shout for joy, sound free-dom's cry; All na-ture sing for she is nigh.
3. Come join hands let us u - nite, Walk- ing to-geth - er in - to light.

1.-3. Christ - So- phi - a now we praise; Joy - ful songs our voic- es raise.

Words © 1996 Jann Aldredge-Clanton

MENDELSSOHN Felix Mendelssohn, 1840;
arrang.William H. Cummings, 1855

5 COME, CHRIST-SOPHIA, HEALING POWER

1. Come, Christ-So - phi - a, heal - ing pow'r; Your grace all earth ex - tols;
2. Come, Christ-So - phi - a, give your hand To wipe our weep - ing eyes;
3. You calm our fears; you ease our pain; You heal our trou - bled hearts.
4. Come, Christ-So - phi - a, pow'r who heals; You make the wound - ed whole;

1. Your touch can make our spir - its flow'r; Your love re - stores our souls.
2. Our sor - rows you can un - der - stand; You feel our deep - est cries.
3. Your voice bids us new life to gain; Your name deep peace im - parts.
4. Your sa - cred name cre - a - tion fills With hope and health and joy.

Words © 1996 Jann Aldredge-Clanton

NEW BRITAIN *Virginia Harmony*, 1831;
arr. Edwin O. Excell, 1851–1921

COME, CHRIST-SOPHIA, OUR WAY 6

(Proverbs 4:11–18; John 14:6, 15:15)

1. Come, Christ-So-phi-a, our way To a more peace - ful day;
2. Come, Christ-So-phi-a, our truth, Wis-dom for age and youth;
3. Come, Christ-So-phi-a, our life; Our deep-est hopes re - vive.
4. Come, Christ-So-phi-a, our friend; Help us our world to mend;

1. Fol - low - ing you, we break op - pres - sion's wall, An - swer - ing
2. Dwell in our hearts; No more from you we hide; May all our
3. With you we grow; Now we can ful - ly bloom, Giv - ing our
4. Fill all our days With love and heal - ing peace, As we our

1. free - dom's call, Clear-ing a path for all To make things new.
2. fears sub - side; Now we with you a - bide, Your word im - part.
3. spir - its room New pow - er to as - sume, Our whole-ness know.
4. gifts re - lease; O may earth's joy in - crease, Now and al - ways.

ITALIAN HYMN Felice de Giardini, 1716–1796

7 COME, HOLY BEAUTY

1. Come, Holy Beauty, stir our full humanity
2. Come, Christ-Sophia, heal all wounded nature
3. Come, Holy Spirit, fill us with your wisdom.
4. Come, Holy Beauty, waken our divinity

1. That we may know we embody you. All our diversity
2. That suffers long in grief and woe, Scarred by our careless hands,
3. Open our eyes that we may see Splendor and holiness
4. That we may be your image fair, Clothed in your dignity,

1. mirrors your truth and grace; All races show your lovely hue.
2. cries out to thrive again, To blossom fresh, your radiance show.
3. in every blade of grass, The smallest creature's majesty.
4. wisdom and liberty, Creative pow'r with you to share.

Words © 1996 Jann Aldredge-Clanton

CRUSADERS' HYMN Silesian folk melody
Schlesische Volkslieder, 1842

COME, THOU FROM WHOM 8
ALL BLESSINGS FLOW

1. Come, Thou from whom all bless - ings flow; Wake us to see more
2. Come, Giv - er of all life and peace; May we join you in
3. Come, Spir - it who makes all things new; Show us your wid - er,

1. than we know. Help us claim all our gifts and
2. Earth's in - crease. Grant us new cour - age for this
3. full - er view. Teach us our whole - ness now to

1. pow'r. Fill us with grace that we may flow'r.
2. day That we may find true Wis - dom's way.
3. see; Stir us to be all we can be.

OLD 100TH attr. Louis Bourgeois, 1510–1561

9 COME TO ME, ALL YOU WITH HEAVY HEARTS

(Matthew 11:28–30, Sirach 6:25, 28)

"Come un-to me, you wea-ry ones, And I will give you rest;
Come, leave your bur-dens in my arms, And lean up-on my breast."

Fine

1. We hear you, Christ-So - phi - a, Our heav - y hearts re - joice
2. We la - bor, Christ-So - phi - a, To bring your truth to light;
3. You call us, Christ-So - phi - a, Our spir - its to re - vive;

D.C. al Fine

1. To bring our cares un - to you, And heed your gen - tle voice.
2. We of - ten feel dis - cour - aged When wrong pre - vails o'er right.
3. We learn from you the wis - dom To keep our hope a - live.

Words © 1996 Jann Aldredge-Clanton

BALM IN GILEAD Negro Spiritual

124

Do You Want to Be Healed? 10

(John 5:2–9)

1. "Do you want to be healed?" calls a voice ten-der-ly; "Do
2. "Rise up, em-brace new life," calls the voice ur-gent-ly; "New
3. We hear your voice with-in, call-ing us, call-ing us; O

1. you want to be healed and made well? If you want to be
2. life is wait-ing for your em-brace. Take up your free-dom
3. Christ-So-phi-a, we hear your voice. Help us to claim your

1. whole, Cast off each crip-pling role; Un-chain your fet-tered soul;
2. now; Your spir-it's growth al-low; Move for-ward in-to your
3. grace, Old pat-terns to e-rase; Your new cre-a-tion's sign,

1. be set free, be set free; Un-chain your fet-tered soul; be set free."
2. full-est wis-dom and health; Move for-ward in-to your full-est self."
3. we will be, we will be; Your new cre-a-tion's sign, we will be.

WONDROUS LOVE William Walker's *Southern Harmony*, 1835;
arr. William J. Reynolds, 1920–

11 GATHER US UNDER YOUR WARM WINGS

(Matthew 23:37)

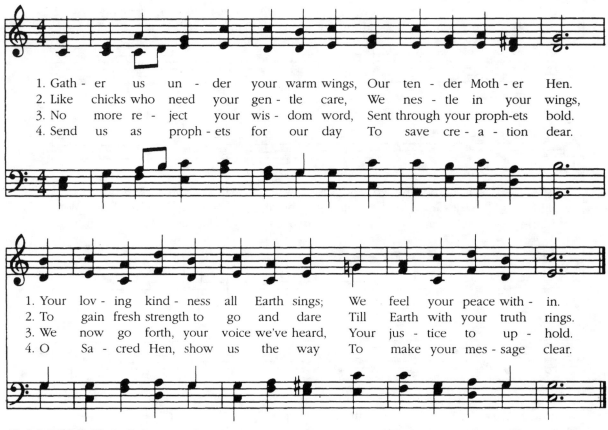

1. Gath - er us un - der your warm wings, Our ten - der Moth - er Hen.
2. Like chicks who need your gen - tle care, We nes - tle in your wings,
3. No more re - ject your wis - dom word, Sent through your proph-ets bold.
4. Send us as proph - ets for our day To save cre - a - tion dear.

1. Your lov - ing kind - ness all Earth sings; We feel your peace with - in.
2. To gain fresh strength to go and dare Till Earth with your truth rings.
3. We now go forth, your voice we've heard, Your jus - tice to up - hold.
4. O Sa - cred Hen, show us the way To make your mes - sage clear.

ST. ANNE William Croft, 1678–1727

1. Holy Christ-So-phi-a, beau-ti-ful Cre-a-tor,
2. Bles-sed Christ-So-phi-a, mer-ci-ful Re-deem-er,
3. Migh-ty Christ-So-phi-a, gen-tle Ho-ly Spir-it,
4. Ho-ly Christ-So-phi-a, trin-i-ty of Wis-dom,

1. Rouse us from our slum-ber-ing to make the world a-new.
2. Heal, re-store, and chal-lenge us to set all cap-tives free.
3. Sis-ters, broth-ers, side by side, join in your work of peace.
4. All cre-a-tion sings your praise in ac-cents wild and free.

1. Ho-ly Christ-So-phi-a, may we join your la-bor
2. You a-lone can save us by your voice with-in us,
3. Ho-ly Christ-So-phi-a, com-fort-ing and guid-ing,
4. Moun-tains bow be-fore you, pur-ple fields ex-tol you

1. To bring forth peace and all that's just and true.
2. Call-ing us on toward all we're meant to be.
3. Give us new hope and pow-er to re-lease.
4. For your pure grace, your true e-qual-i-ty.

Words © 1996 Jann Aldredge-Clanton   NICAEA John B. Dykes, 1823–1876

13 HOPE OF GLORY, LIVING IN US

(Colossians 1:27; Romans 8:18–25; Proverbs 13:12)

1. Hope of glo - ry, liv - ing in us, Christ-So - phi - a, you we praise.
2. Hope de - ferred makes hearts grow heav - y, Christ-So - phi - a, help us wait;
3. All cre - a - tion stands on tip - toe, long - ing toward re - veal - ing light;
4. Gra - cious liv - ing, hope of glo - ry, Christ-So - phi - a, you we bless;

1. By your name we gain fresh cour - age, strength to dare new trails to blaze.
2. Keep our vi - sions plain be - fore us so re - solve will not a - bate.
3. Hope sus - tains the glo - rious mys - t'ry, till our faith turns in - to sight.
4. Voice of wis - dom deep with - in us, with your word our souls re - fresh.

1. May we feel your stir - ring Spir - it, lead - ing us as on we go;
2. Chal-lenged by your res - ur - rec - tion, we find hope to make things new;
3. Look, there springs a heal - ing riv - er, flow - ing by a tree of life;
4. Joy - ful res - ur - rec - tion sto - ry, mir - a - cle for all to claim,

1. Bring - ing change ful - fills our call - ing, though the way seems long and slow.
2. Now de - sire will find ful - fill - ment, as new life comes in - to view.
3. Quench-ing thirst for peace and jus - tice, all Earth's splen - dor to re - vive.
4. May we rise to full - est beau - ty by the pow - er of your name.

HYFRYDOL Rowland H. Prichard, 1831

LET JUSTICE LIKE WATERS ROLL DOWN 14

(Amos 5:24; Luke 4:18)

1. Let jus-tice like wa-ters roll down on our land;
2. Pure wis-dom and jus-tice flow forth from your hand;
3. Come now, Christ-So-phi-a, with bless-ings and peace
4. O may we flow free-ly like wa-ters and streams

1. Help us, Christ-So-phi-a, to join in your plan.
2. With you as our guide e-vil forc-es dis-band.
3. To calm us and stir us our vi-sions re-lease,
4. To heal and re-store bro-ken hearts and lost dreams.

1. Let right-eous-ness like ev-er-flow-ing streams rise;
2. Give us, Christ-So-phi-a, the grace to pre-vail
3. Good news for the poor and fresh sight for the blind;
4. A-wak-en us ful-ly to all we can be,

1. Come fill and a-noint us, O Spir-it most wise.
2. O'er sys-tems and pow-ers that keep cap-tives held.
3. Your voice calls us on the op-pressed to un-bind.
4. Re-claim-ing our souls as we set peo-ple free.

ST. DENIO Welsh folk melody

15 LOVE RISES UP

(Hebrews 2:2-3; Luke 24:46-47)

1. Love ris-es up from dead-ly foes, Heal-ing di-
2. Hope springs from vi-sions plain to see, Set-ting op-
3. Joy blos-soms free-ly through all lands; Sis-ters and

1. vi-sions pain, and woes; Our great Cre-a-tor-
2. pres-sive sys-tems free; Our ris-en Sis-ter-
3. broth-ers, hand in hand, Bring new cre-a-tion's

1. Wis-dom - Guide Leads to new life so full and wide.
2. Broth-er - Friend Gives us new pow'r, our world to mend.
3. dream to sight, Ris-ing to-geth-er in-to light.

DUKE STREET John Hatton, c. 1720–1793

New Miracles Unfold 16

(Psalm 89:5; 2 Corinthians 5:17)

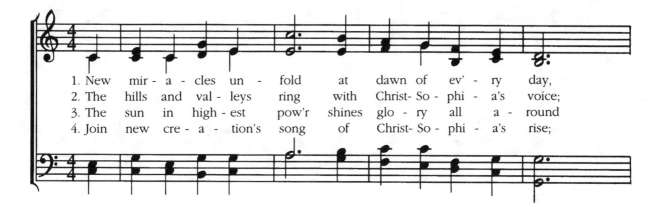

1. New mir-a-cles un-fold at dawn of ev'-ry day,
2. The hills and val-leys ring with Christ-So-phi-a's voice;
3. The sun in high-est pow'r shines glo-ry all a-round
4. Join new cre-a-tion's song of Christ-So-phi-a's rise;

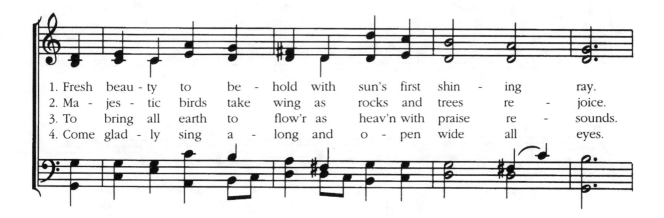

1. Fresh beau-ty to be-hold with sun's first shin-ing ray.
2. Ma-jes-tic birds take wing as rocks and trees re-joice.
3. To bring all earth to flow'r as heav'n with praise re-sounds.
4. Come glad-ly sing a-long and o-pen wide all eyes.

1.-4. A-wake and see, a-wake and see The whole world bloom with won-ders free.

Words © 1996 Jann Aldredge-Clanton   DARWALL John Darwall, 1770

17 O Blessed Christ-Sophia

(Isaiah 53:3; John 12:12–16)

1. O bless-ed Christ-So - phi - a, to you we lift our praise;
2. You en - ter hum-ble set - tings and grace com-mu - ni - ties,
3. Now make tri - um-phal en - try in - to our minds and souls;
4. Most Ho - ly Christ-So - phi - a, O wise and bless-ed one,

1. In grate - ful ad - o - ra - tion, our voic - es now we raise.
2. Re - ceive a roy - al wel - come from eve - ry-one who sees;
3. O bless - ed Christ-So - phi - a, in - spire our dreams and goals.
4. To you we sing ho - san - nas, your vic - to - ry is won.

1. Too long your name and im - age we've hid - den from our eyes;
2. O bless - ed Christ-So - phi - a, you come in eve - ry age,
3. O may we catch your vi - sion of part - ner - ship and peace,
4. The palm trees wave their branch - es to cel - e - brate your reign;

1. Too long your words of wis - dom, re - ject - ed and de - spised.
2. Un - set - tling priest and proph - et, sur - pris - ing wis - est sage.
3. Trans - form - ing all our la - bor, our tal - ents to re - lease.
4. We dance in ex - pec - ta - tion of whole - ness to re - gain.

Words © 1996 Jann Aldredge-Clanton

ST. THEODULPH Melchior Teschner, 1584–1635

O Christ-Sophia, Be Born in Us 18

(Isaiah 9:2–4; Luke 1:52–53, 2:10–14)

1. O Christ - So-phi- a, be born in us, we need your pow'r and grace;
2. O Christ - So-phi- a, your ra - diant life shines through the win - ter's night;
3. O Christ - So-phi- a, come dwell in us, for you our spir - its long;

1. En - cour- age us to la - bor long in - jus - tice to e - rase.
2. Your ten- der touch re - stores our souls and brings new truth to sight.
3. In - spire our dreams and stir our hopes with bless - ed an - gels' song:

1. Come help us break op- pres-sion's yoke and end the bit - ter strife;
2. A - wak - en us to change our world, your im - age ful - ly show,
3. "Fear not, be- hold the peace-ful land where dawns a glo- ri - ous morn;

1. Lift up the low - ly, poor, and weak to fresh, a - bun - dant life.
2. All wom- en, men, and chil - dren free to love, cre-ate, and grow.
3. Good news of joy to all the earth, for Christ- So-phi-a is born."

Words © 1996 Jann Aldredge-Clanton   CAROL Richard Storrs Willis, 1819–1900

19 O Come, Christ-Sophia

1. O come, Christ-So - phi - a, full of grace and wis - dom; Come bless us, come
2. We long for your com - ing, la - bor for your birth - ing, For you are our
3. Re - joice all you peo - ple, sis - ters, broth - ers, join now To sing of a

1. chal-lenge us to make life a - new. Come bring us pow - er, beau - ty, hope, and
2. hope of peace, our pow - er for change. Come Christ-So - phi - a, break down walls and
3. bright new day just dawn-ing for all. Sing now a new song, sing with ju - bi -

1. har - mo - ny.
2. free us. 1.-3. O come, thou Christ-So- phi - a, O come, thou Christ-So - phi - a,
3. la - tion.

1.-4. O come, thou Christ-So - phi - a, wis - dom and peace.

Words © 1996 Jann Aldredge-Clanton

ADESTE FIDELES John Francis Wade, c. 1711–1786

O COME, JOIN HANDS, ALL VIOLENCE CEASE 20

(Luke 19:42; Ephesians 2:14; Proverbs 3:13–17; Isaiah 55:12)

1. O come join hands, all vio - lence cease, And fol - low Christ-So-
2. Come heal di - vi - sions, break down walls, And lis - ten to the
3. Come wom - en, men, and chil - dren now; As part - ners make a
4. The moun - tains and the hills shall sing, When peace through-out the

1. phi - a, our peace, Who bids us o - pen eyes to see The
2. Spir - it's calls To heal op - pres - sive sys - tems' blight, So
3. sa - cred vow To fol - low Wis - dom's paths to peace, And
4. world takes wing; The trees shall clap their hands in glee, As

1. ways that we make peace to be.
2. peace breaks through to give new sight. 1.-3. A - rise, a - rise, feel
3. teach her ways of full re - lease.
4. joy bursts forth o'er land and sea.

1.-3. joy in - crease; Come fol - low Christ - So - phi - a, our peace.

Words © 1996 Jann Aldredge-Clanton

VENI EMMANUEL Plainsong;
adapt. Thomas Helmore, 1811–1890

21 O Flower Blooming in Deepest Pain

(Song of Songs 1:5–7, 2:1–2)

1. O Flow-er bloom-ing in deep-est pain, Sti - fled, ne-
2. Flow-er So - phi - a of rich-est hue, Come-ly and
3. Rise from the dust of sa - cred page; In - to our
4. Lil - y So - phi - a, pure de - light, O Rose of

1. glect - ed, cursed, and scorned; Lil - y of black your
2. dark your im - age sur - vives; No e - vil force your
3. world bloom fresh and free. Flow-er So - phi - a from
4. Shar - on, you in - spire Cour - age to speak for

1. beau - ty has lain Bur - ied in veils, passed by, for - lorn.
2. pow'r can sub - due; Though oft cast down your Spir - it thrives.
3. age to age, O - pen our eyes your full - ness to see.
4. truth and right, Faith to ful - fill our soul's de - sire.

Words © 1996 Jann Aldredge-Clanton

HAMBURG Lowell Mason, 1792–1872

O Holy Darkness, Loving Womb 22

(Psalm 139:12; Isaiah 45:3)

1. O Ho-ly Dark-ness, lov-ing womb, who nur-tures and cre-ates,
2. Cre-a-tive Dark-ness, clos-est friend, you whis-per in the night;
3. O Ho-ly Night of deep-est bliss, we cel-e-brate your pow'r;
4. O Ho-ly Christ-So-phi-a, your im-age black and fair,

1. Sus-tain us through the long-est night with dreams of o-pen gates.
2. You calm our fears as un-known paths sur-prise us with new sight.
3. In-fuse us with your en-er-gy that brings our seeds to flow'r.
4. Stirs us to end in-jus-tice and the wounds of Earth re-pair.

1. We move in-side to mys-t'ry that in our cen-ter dwells,
2. We mar-vel at your boun-ty, your gifts so full and free,
3. The voice out of the dark-ness ex-cites our warm-est zeal
4. The treas-ures of your dark-ness and rich-es of your grace

1. Where streams of rich-est beau-ty flow from sa-cred, liv-ing wells.
2. Un-fold-ing as you wak-en us to new re-al-i-ty.
3. To bring to-geth-er dark and light, true ho-li-ness re-veal.
4. In-spire us to ful-fill our call, our sa-cred-ness em-brace.

Words © 1996 Jann Aldredge-Clanton

ST. LOUIS Lewis H. Redner, 1831–1908

23 O Mother Rock Who Bore Us

(Deuteronomy 32:18)

1. O Moth-er Rock who bore us, un-mind-ful we have been
2. Our world cries out in an-guish from our ne-glect of you,
3. Teach us to be more mind-ful, O Rock who gave us birth,

1. Of all your good-ness to us, your mer-cy with-out end.
2. O Moth-er Rock who bore us, come now our souls re-new.
3. Re-flect-ing on your beau-ty that per-me-ates the earth.

1. We've praised our Fa-ther ful-ly, but scorned your im-age fair,
2. For-give our long for-get-ting of your strong, lov-ing care;
3. Re-store our child-like won-der, as we up-on you gaze,

1. Re-ject-ing all your wis-dom that shines forth ev'-ry-where.
2. O may we now dis-cov-er your gifts for all to share.
3. And may we give you glad-ly, our songs of end-less praise.

Words © 1996 Jann Aldredge-Clanton

PASSION CHORALE Hans Leo Hassler, 1564–1612;
harm. Johann Sebastian Bach,1685–1750

Out of the Depths Christ-Sophia Is Calling 24

1. Out of the depths Christ-So-phi-a is call-ing, Call-ing from
2. Long have we la-bored and hun-gered for bless-ing, Bless-ing of
3. Deep in our souls Christ-So-phi-a is long-ing, Long-ing to
4. Come and re-ceive Christ-So-phi-a's rich bless-ings, Bless-ings for

1. deep in our souls; Gent-ly the voice of true wis-dom and heal-ing
2. all we can be, While all a-long our true voice has been call-ing,
3. calm all our fears, Com-fort our griev-ing and share all our strug-gles,
4. you and for me, Peace for our jour-ney and hope for our vi-sion,

1. Calls us to rise and be whole.
2. Call-ing in you and in me. 1.-4. "Come home,   come home,"
3. Wip-ing a-way eve-ry tear.
4. Cour-age to set us all free.

1.-4. Hear Christ-So-phi-a's clear call; "Come to your full-ness of

1.-4. pow-er and wis-dom; Come home to life with-in you."

THOMPSON Will L. Thompson, 1847–1909

25 Praise Ruah,* Spirit Who Gives Birth

(Genesis 1)

1. Praise Ru - ah, Spir - it who gives birth To worlds un - known and life on earth.
2. Day dawns at sound of Ru - ah's voice; Wake all cre - a - tion to re - joice:
3. Tall trees in red and gold - en dress And rip - ened fruits their Mak - er bless:
4. Cold winds and drifts of ic - y snow Part us from all that we would know.
5. Fresh tu - lips lift their crim - son cups; Hope new -born in the heart leaps up;

1. O praise her! Hal- le- lu - jah! Stars danc- ing mys - t'ry through the night
2. O praise her! Hal- le- lu - jah! Sun gleams like dia - monds on the dew;
3. O praise her! Hal- le- lu - jah! Come now and gath - er har - vest home;
4. O praise her! Hal- le- lu - jah! Each soul a - waits in slum - ber deep
5. O praise her! Hal- le- lu - jah! Wild - flow- ers ris - ing in - to view

1. Show forth her joy and end - less light. Praise Ru - ah! Hal- le- lu - jah!
2. Birds join to sing the hymn a - new: Praise Ru - ah! Hal- le- lu - jah!
3. All be - ings feel a deep sha - lom. Praise Ru - ah! Hal- le- lu - jah!
4. Her warm- ing love to wake from sleep. Praise Ru - ah! Hal- le- lu - jah!
5. Cloth fer - tile fields in rain - bow hue; Praise Ru - ah! Hal- le- lu - jah!

1.-5. Praise the great cre - a - tive Spir - it! Come and praise her!

LASST UNS ERFREUEN *Geistliche Kirchengesäng*, 1623

*Hebrew word for "Spirit," pronounced ru'akh ("ch" as in Scottish "loch")

1. Rise up, O Christ-Sophia, for you the whole world longs
2. Lead on, O Queen of Wisdom; we need you more than e'er.
3. Guide us, thou Christ-Sophia, on paths of truth and light.

1. With eager expectation, till you shall right our wrongs.
2. You are the truth within us; you shine through all that's fair.
3. Creation yearns for freedom in your pure beauty bright.

1. Your gentle words of wisdom, your warm caress of peace.
2. Our hearts cry out for justice midst conflict, pain, and strife;
3. You call us as your ministers, to serve with you on earth,

1. Empower us to labor with you our wars to cease.
2. You calm the raging tempests to bring us peace and life.
3. To co-create a myst'ry, new life with you to birth.

Words © 1996 Jann Aldredge-Clanton

LANCASHIRE Henry T. Smart, 1813–1879

141

27 Rise Up, O People, Proclaim Christ-Sophia Has Risen

(Isaiah 60:1–5; Matthew 9:22)

1. Rise up, O peo-ple, pro-claim Christ-So-phi-a has ris - en, Rais-ing the bur - ied and op'n-ing the doors to all pris - ons. Rise up and shine! Light-ing the path - way di - vine, As we de - clare this true vi - sion.
2. Take heart, O daugh-ters, be-hold, Christ-So-phi-a brings heal - ing; Sons, lift your eyes and find health in this sa - cred re - veal - ing. Claim life a - new! Earth's rich-est beau - ty re - new, Show-ing a way so ap - peal - ing.
3. Come now, O sis-ters, and join Christ-So-phi-a in dar - ing, Broth-ers, join in and lay down heav-y bur - dens you're bear - ing. Come one and all! Fol - low the life - giv - ing call, Chang-ing the world through deep car - ing.
4. Sing a new song and re - joice, Christ-So-phi-a a - dor - ing, Glo - ry and free - dom with - in and a - round us re - stor - ing. Sing, for the light Comes to re - vive truth and right; Now ra - diant spir - its are soar - ing.

Words © 1996 Jann Aldredge-Clanton

LOBE DEN HERREN *Stralsund Gesangbuch*, 1665
harm. W. Sterndale Bennett, 1816–1875

Send Us Forth, O Christ-Sophia 28

(Matthew 25:35–40; Matthew 5:13; Luke 13:20–21)

1. Send us forth, O Christ-So - phi - a, on your mis-sion in your name;
2. May we see you, Christ-So - phi - a, all a - round us eve - ry - where,
3. For your mis - sion, Christ-So - phi - a, give us in - sight, hope, and grace;
4. Christ-So - phi - a, you have called us, your great mis-sion to ful - fill;

1. Fill us with your lov - ing wis - dom, all your jus - tice to pro - claim.
2. In our sis - ters and our broth-ers hurt - ing for some - one to care.
3. May we see all liv - ing be - ings as re - flect - ing your bright face.
4. Grant us faith to go forth bold - ly, your just vi - sion to make real.

1. Help us change op - pres - sive sys - tems, lib - er - at - ing all with - in,
2. As we do for those who suf - fer, we do al - so un - to you,
3. Sis - ter Earth cries out in an - guish with all oth - ers last and least;
4. When our spir - its sag and fal - ter, give us hope to keep a - live,

1. Break-ing walls and build - ing bridg-es, right -ing wrongs, re - deem-ing sin.
2. Join - ing hands with one an - oth- er, we work to make all things new.
3. By re - stor - ing her rich beau - ty, we be - come the salt and yeast.
4. Cour-age to change words and ac - tions, all cre - a - tion to re - vive.

BEECHER John Zundel, 1815–1882

29 SHARE OUR GRIEF, O CHRIST-SOPHIA

(Psalm 30:5; 2 Corinthians 1:3–5; Revelation 21:4)

1. Share our grief, O Christ-So-phi - a; Hear our cries and feel our pain.
2. Wipe our tears, O Christ-So-phi - a, Heal our wounds, as - suage our grief.
3. Give us now, O Christ-So-phi - a, Kind - ness and con - sol - ing grace.

1. Sor - row's clouds hang dark a - round us; Heav - y tears flow down like rain.
2. Death and mourn-ing will be o - ver; Cry - ing eyes will find re - lief.
3. As we share your ten - der com - fort, We be - hold your bless - ed face.

1.-3. Weep-ing en-dures while the long night pass - es; Joy dawns a - gain with the morn - ing light.

1.-3. New life blooms through dust and ash - es; Hope re - born, we gain fresh sight.

Words © 1996 Jann Aldredge-Clanton   RESTORATION William Walker's *Southern Harmony*, 1835

Stir Us Out of Our Safe Nest, 30
Mother Eagle

(Deuteronomy 32:11–12)

1. Stir us out of our safe nest; Moth-er Ea-gle,
2. Take us up on your strong wings; Moth-er Ea-gle,
3. Moth-er Ea-gle, send us out, Free-ly fly-ing
4. As with ea-gle's wings we fly, Leav-ing each con-

1. come near-by. Hold us close to your warm breast,
2. give us flight; Borne a-loft our spir-its sing,
3. on our own. Claim-ing all our gifts we shout,
4. fin-ing place. For fresh air and forms we cry,

1. While we learn to risk and fly. Lift us up with
2. As we soar in-to your light. Lift us up with
3. Glad to be at last full grown. Soar-ing now with
4. As we move out in-to space. Soar-ing now with

1. you, we pray; Help us see a bright new day.
2. you, we pray; Help us see a bright new day.
3. you, we say, "Look, there dawns the bright new day."
4. you, we say, "Look, there dawns the bright new day."

Words © 1996 Jann Aldredge-Clanton

DIX Conrad Kocher, 1786–1872;
adapt. William Henry Monk, 1823–1889

31 TREAD LIGHTLY ON YOUR HEAVY PATH

(Psalm 23)

(A solo voice sings the first two lines of each stanza; all sing the last two lines.)

1. "Tread light-ly on your heav-y path; your spir-it can stay free;
2. "Tread gen-tly through the wea-ry maze; stay calm-ly clear and whole.
3. "Tread smooth-ly on the rug-ged edge; your strength will long en-dure;

1. Walk soft-ly past the fear and wrath; there's more in life to see."
2. With mead-ows green sur-round your days; deep peace re-stores your soul."
3. Move sure-ly o'er each crag and ledge; your steps will be se-cure."

1. We hear your gen-tle voice with-in, O Christ-So-phi-a, Friend;
2. We hear you, Christ-So-phi-a, Friend; for you our spir-its long;
3. Your words of com-fort light our way; O Christ-So-phi-a, Guide;

1. You lead us past the nois-y din, by wa-ters still you wend.
2. Your voice bids us our needs to tend; you fill our lives with song.
3. Your kind-ness o-ver-flows each day, as we with you a-bide.

Words © 1996 Jann Aldredge-Clanton

RESIGNATION *Southern Harmony*, 1835

We Claim Your Support, 32
Christ-Sophia, Our Rock

(1 Corinthians 10:4; Isaiah 51:1)

1. We claim your sup - port, Christ- So - phi - a, our Rock;
2. O Rock of Cre - a - tion, from you we were made;
3. O Rock that is high - er than all of our dreams,
4. Cast out all our fears, Christ- So - phi - a, we pray;

1. Your life - giv - ing pow - ers our treas - ures un - lock.
2. We mir - ror your im - age which nev - er shall fade.
3. From depths of your beau - ty come free- flow - ing streams;
4. We call on your strength to cre - ate a new day.

1. Our tal - ents and grac - es re - store wea - ry land;
2. You nour - ish our gifts with your spir - i - tual flow;
3. We drink from your well of deep wis - dom and peace;
4. O Rock of Sal - va - tion, on you we de - pend;

1. O sol - id foun - da - tion, on you we can stand.
2. You strength - en our steps as new path - ways we show.
3. Your wa - ter of life brings cre - a - tive re - lease.
4. Your good - ness and kind - ness spring forth with - out end.

Words © 1996 Jann Aldredge-Clanton   FOUNDATION Joseph Funk's *Genuine Church Music*, 1832

33 WE GIVE THANKS TO YOU, DEAR EARTH

(Proverbs 4:11, 6:6–8; Wisdom 8:1)

1. We give thanks to you, dear Earth, For your gifts so
2. Love-ly Earth, your glo-ry fills Laugh-ing brooks and
3. All your life deep val-ue holds; Small-est ants teach
4. Hear, O Earth, our sol-emn vow To con-serve your

1. rich and rare, For new life you bring to birth,
2. flow'r-ing trees, Soar-ing birds o'er gold-en hills,
3. wis-dom's way; Work-ing hard they share all loads,
4. sa-cred life, Car-ing for your fu-ture now,

1. Teach-ing us your ten-der care. May we nur-ture
2. Danc-ing deer so wild and free. May we nur-ture
3. E-qual part-ners eve-ry day. May we join them
4. So your won-ders will sur-vive. May we nur-ture

1. you each day; Christ-So-phi-a guides our way.
2. you each day; Christ-So-phi-a guides our way.
3. as we say Christ-So-phi-a guides our way.
4. you each day; Christ-So-phi-a guides our way.

Words © 1996 Jann Aldredge-Clanton

DIX Conrad Kocher, 1786–1872;
adapt. William Henry Monk, 1823–1889

WE SOUND A CALL TO FREEDOM 34

(Isaiah 58:6–8; John 8:32)

1. We sound a call to free-dom that will heal our bro-ken land; As the
2. We are tired of i-dle prom-is-es and to-ken words and deeds; We want
3. Our re-cov-er-y is com-ing as our eyes re-ceive new sight; We are
* 4. Now our joy breaks forth in dawn-ing of a free and glo-rious day, And our

1. call rings out more clear-ly, vio-lent forc-es will dis-band. Pris-on doors will
2. e-qual rights and ben-e-fits for eve-ry race and creed. Cries of wom-en,
3. mov-ing out of bond-age; we are bound for free-dom bright. As we claim our
4. heal-ing springs up quick-ly as our tal-ents we dis-play. Come and join our

1. o-pen; bonds will loos-en by the Spir-it's hand; The truth will set us free.
2. men, and chil-dren we want eve-ry-one to heed; The truth will set us free.
3. full-est pow-ers, we walk on in-to the light; The truth will set us free.
4. cel-e-bra-tion; come re-joice and glad-ly say; The truth has set us free.

1.-4. Free at last, O Hal-le-lu-jah! Free at last, O Hal-le-lu-jah!

1.-4. Christ-So-phi-a, you have freed us! Your truth has set us free.

Words © 1996 Jann Aldredge-Clanton

BATTLE HYMN American Folk Song, 19th Century

Begin stanza 4 slowly and softly, gradually increasing speed and volume

149

35 WELCOME OUR SISTER-BROTHER CREATOR

1. Come let us join our Sis - ter Cre - a - tor, Birth - ing a
2. Come let us join our Broth - er Cre - a - tor, Bring - ing forth
3. Wel - come our Sis - ter - Broth - er Cre - a - tor, In - to our

1. new world more than we know. With her re - veal - ing
2. free - dom for eve - ry race. All of earth's col - ors
3. spir - its' life - giv - ing wombs. Glad ex - pec - ta - tion

1. all of our full - ness, We cre - ate heal - ing wher - e'er we go.
2. danc - ing to - geth - er, Cel - e - brate beau - ty in eve - ry face.
3. grows from our la - bor For new cre - a - tion's glo - ri - ous blooms.

Words © 1996 Jann Aldredge-Clanton

BUNESSAN Traditional Gaelic melody

WHAT WONDROUS THING 36

(Jeremiah 31:22)

1. What won-drous thing is happ'n-ing here Where minds and souls are op'n-ing?
2. A new thing springs forth on the earth, With bless-ing, hope, and heal-ing;
3. E - piph - a - ny sur-rounds us now, As we re-claim our whole-ness,

1. The scales fall off our blind-ed eyes; New sight a-rous-es hop - ing.
2. The pow'r of wom-an saves all life, So - phi - a-Christ re-veal - ing.
3. So - phi - a-Christ with-in us all, In - spires us with new bold - ness.

1.-4. Look, look, for She is here; Her wis-dom words have long been near.

1.-4. Now, now, be-hold Her grace, Di - vin-i - ty in Her im - age.

Words © 1996 Jann Aldredge-Clanton

GREENSLEEVES Traditional English melody, 16th Century;
harm. John Stainer, 1840–1901

Of Related Interest...

In Search of the Christ-Sophia
An Inclusive Christology for Liberating Christians
Jann Aldredge-Clanton
The author presents an inclusive christology based on the biblical parallel between Christ and Sophia (Wisdom) that will help Christians expand their horizons and rethink traditional beliefs. Powerfully insightful, this book will prepare the reader to understand Christ-Sophia as a way of knowing God in our changing world.

ISBN: 0-89622-629-8, 192 pp, $14.95

Christianity and Feminism in Conversation
Regina A. Coll
In every paragraph the author calls on readers to revise and reclaim the symbols, myths and metaphors of Christianity from a feminist perspective. Maria Harris calls this the book she would select to give an overview of Christian/Catholic feminist theology. No wonder it won first place in Catholic Press Association Book Awards. Comes with excellent questions for reflection.

ISBN: 0-89622-579-8, 208 pp, $14.95

The Hope for Wholeness
A Spirituality for Feminists
Katherine Zappone
Emphasizes the necessity for women to develop relationships with themselves, others, God and nature in order to find a wholeness and completeness in their lives. The author discusses dualism, self-integrity, mutuality, stewardship of the earth, and a fascinating re-definition of sacred symbols. Popular as a text for college women. Includes feminist ritual material.

ISBN: 0-89622-495-3, 208 pp, $12.95

Women in the Middle
Facing Midlife Challenges with Faith
Margot Hover
Guides women through their middle years and reveals the unsung pleasant aspects of middle age. Antoinette Bosco calls this "a gem of a book, like a visit from a friend." Margot Hover captures the essence of the middle years of a woman's life and inspires readers to move forward with acceptance, gratitude and courage.

ISBN: 0-89622-612-3, 88 pp, $7.95

WomanGifts
Biblical Models for Forming Church
Pamela Smith
Illustrations by Virginia DeWan
Each of the portraits in the book introduces the reader to first century Christian women who can be role models for the ministry tasks of women in today's church. Includes prayers and questions for reflection or discussion.

ISBN: 0-89622-572-0, 144 pp, $9.95

Religious Life in the 21st Century
A Contemporary Journey into Canaan
Catherine M. Harmer
This book draws an analogy between the journey of religious communities today and the journey of the Israelites to Canaan and sees both as journeys of faith and trust. Offers practical suggestions for making changes today to become a truly renewed, new model of religious life and church.

ISBN: 0-98622-651-4, 152 pp, $9.95

Available at religious bookstores or from:

TWENTY-THIRD PUBLICATIONS
P.O. Box 180 • Mystic, CT 06355

For a complete list of quality books and videos call:
1 - 8 0 0 - 3 2 1 - 0 4 1 1